I0477557

Catological Coloring Book For Cat Lovers

50 unique full-page designs for hours of cat coloring!

GET 5 BONUS PAGES FREE!

Visit **www.catological.com/coloring-bonus**
to claim your 5 free bonus coloring pages

Catological

ISBN-13: 978-1981104635
ISBN-10: 1981104631

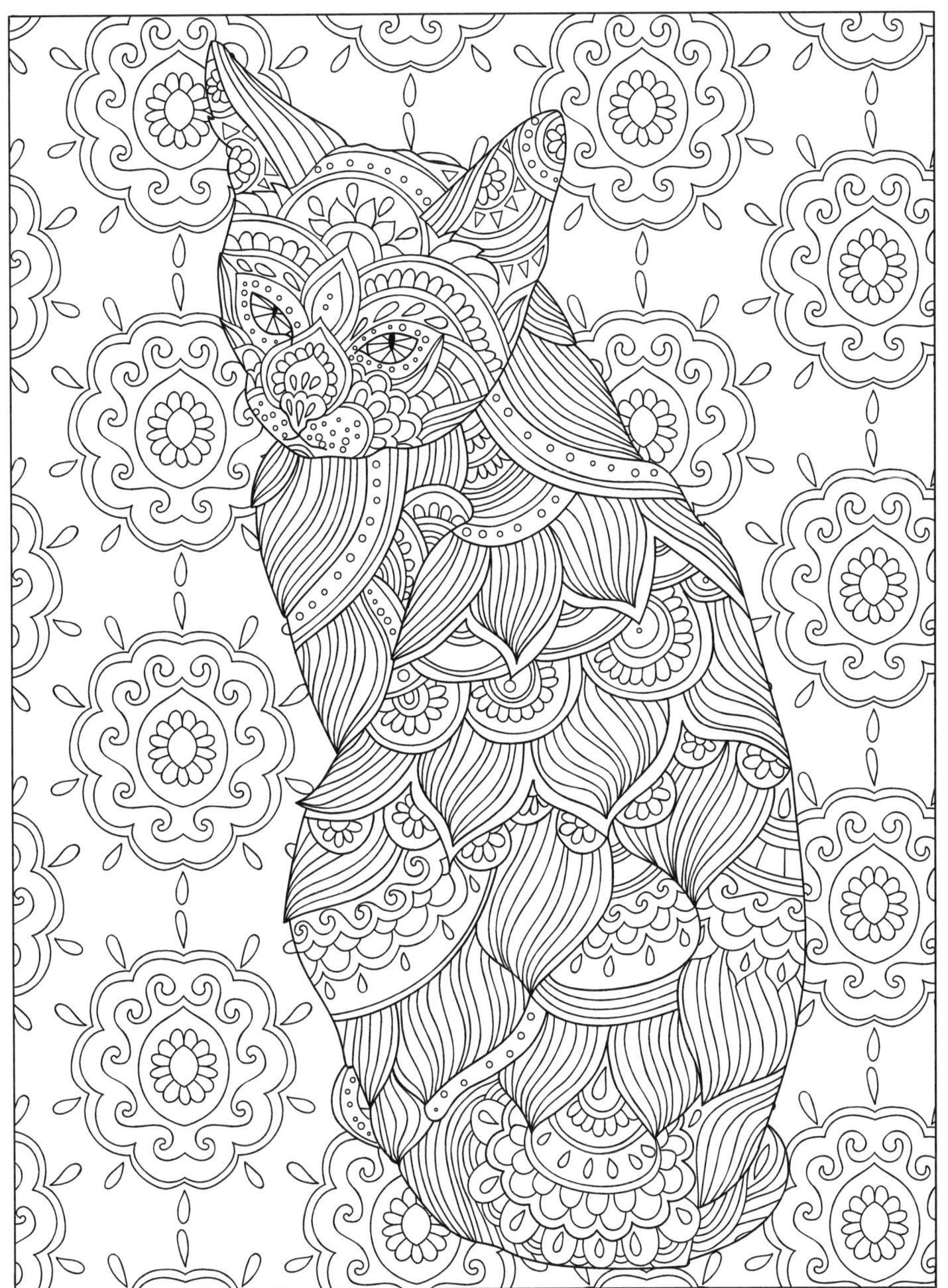

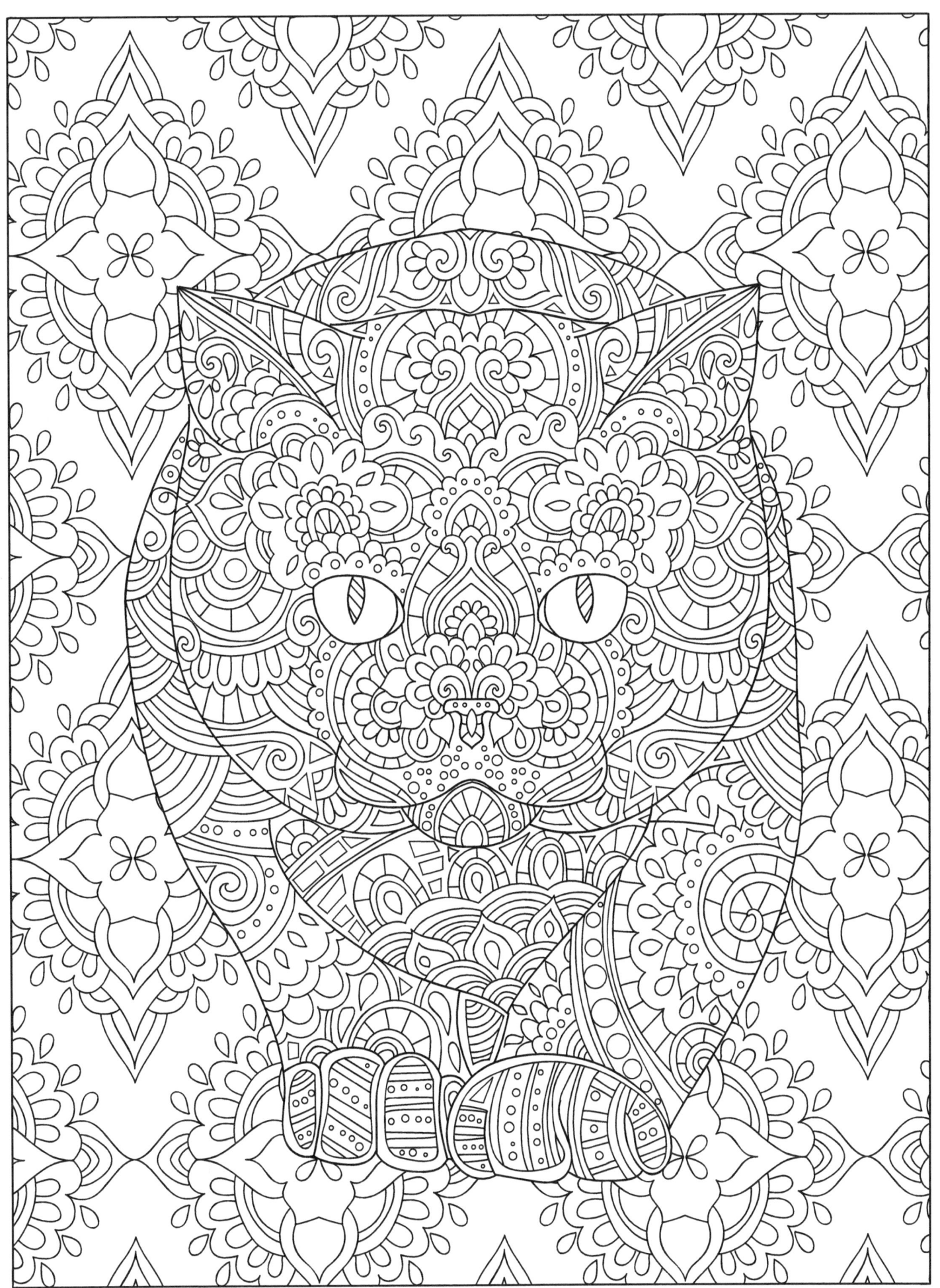

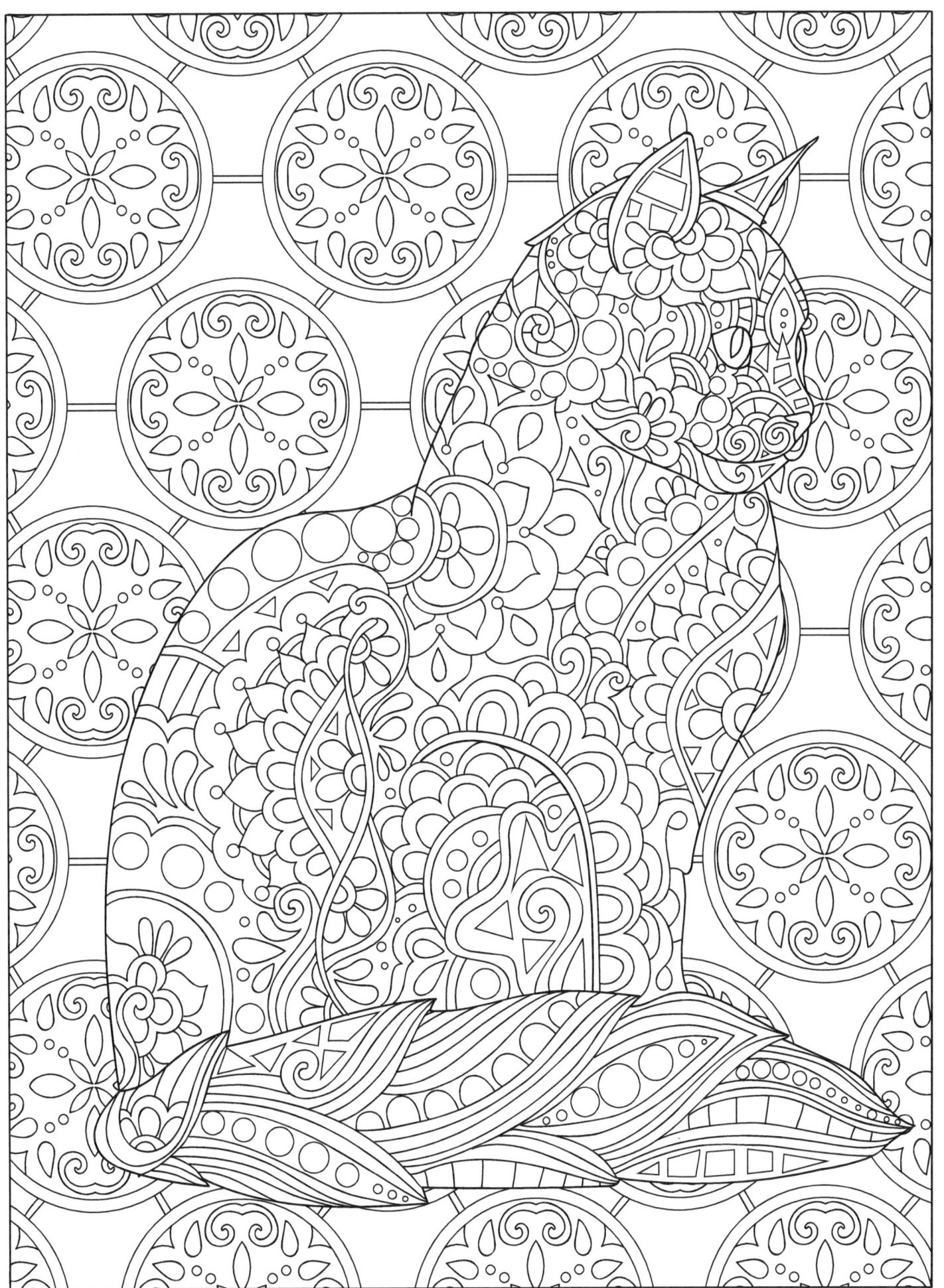

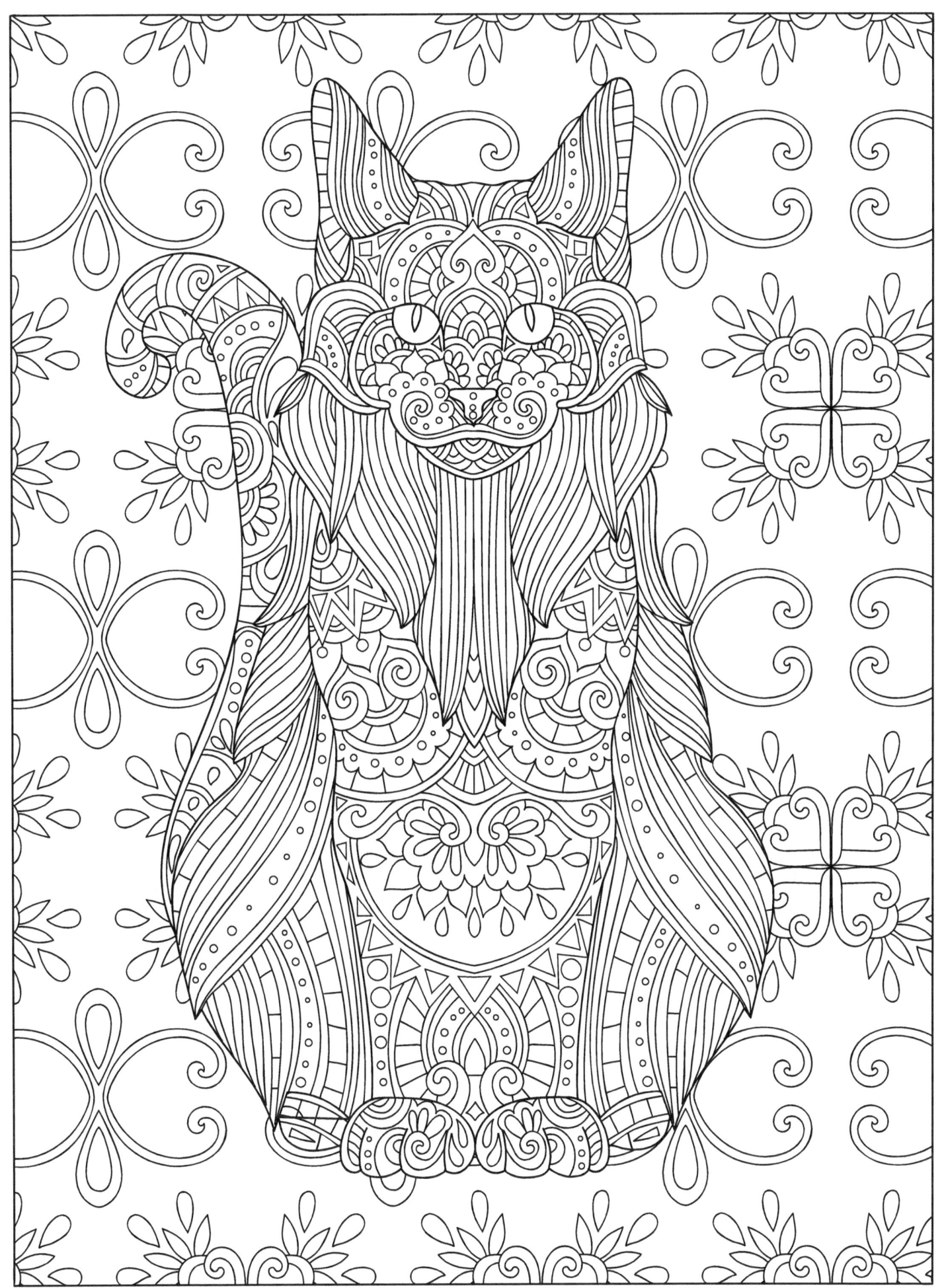

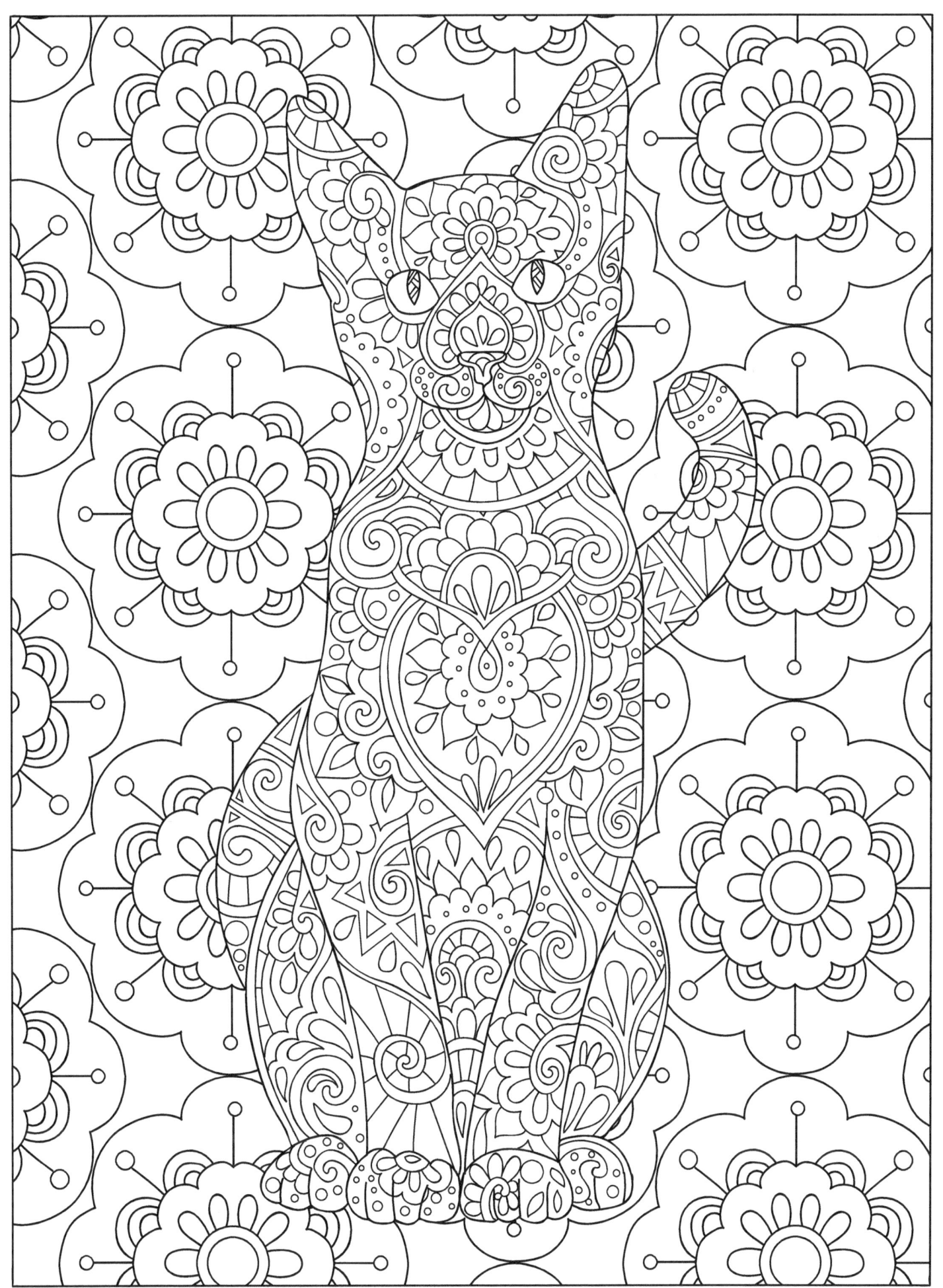

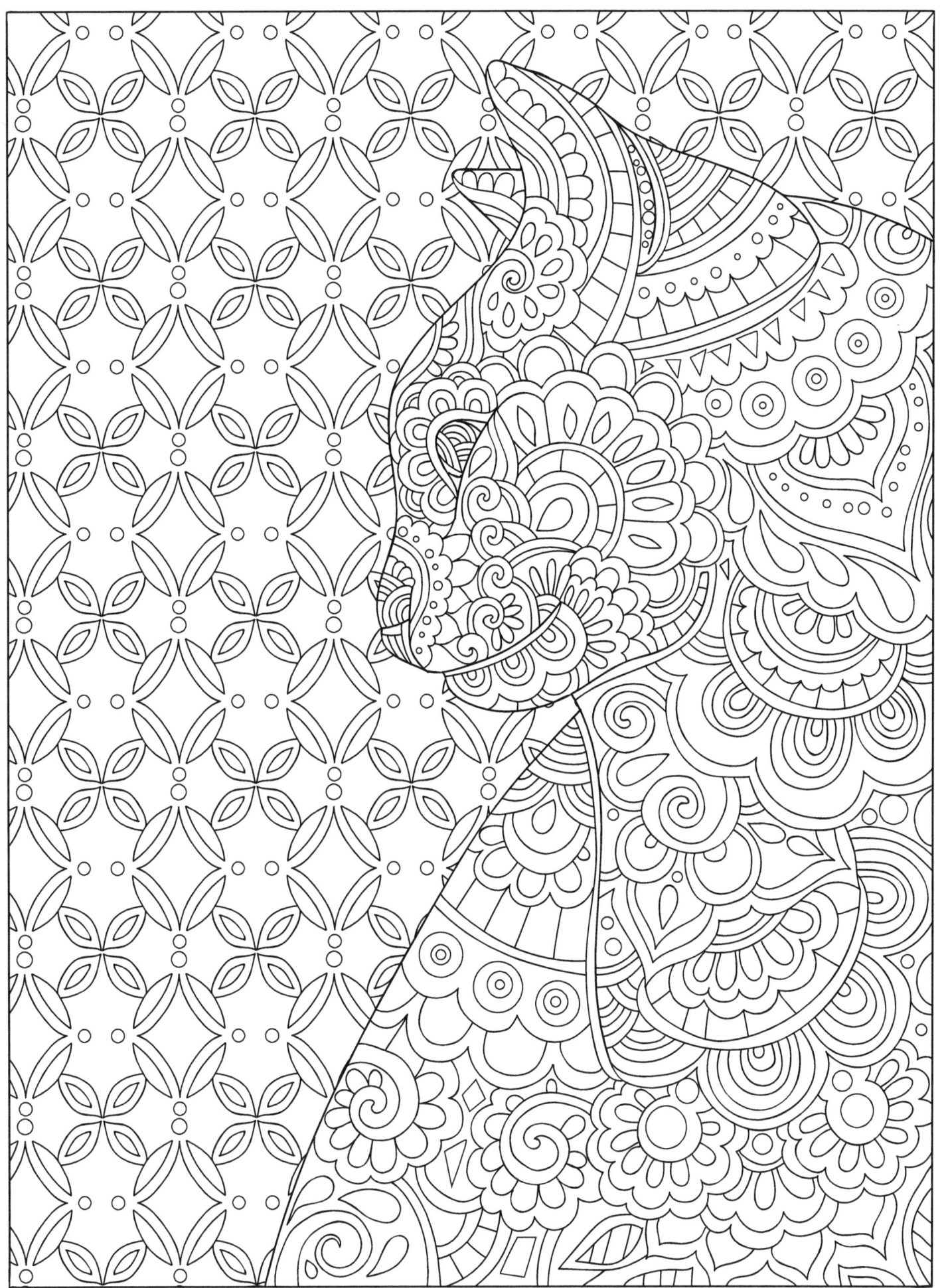

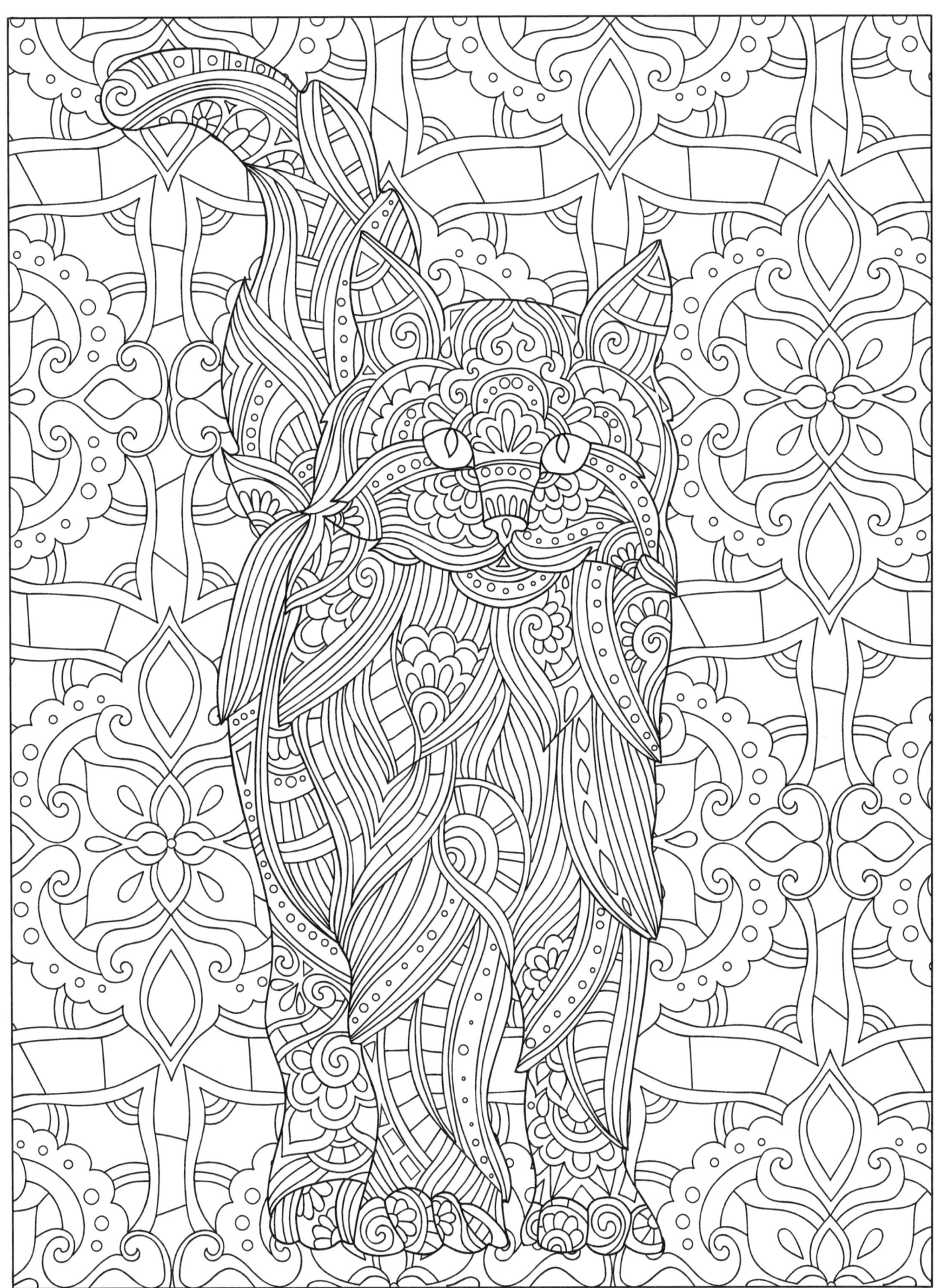

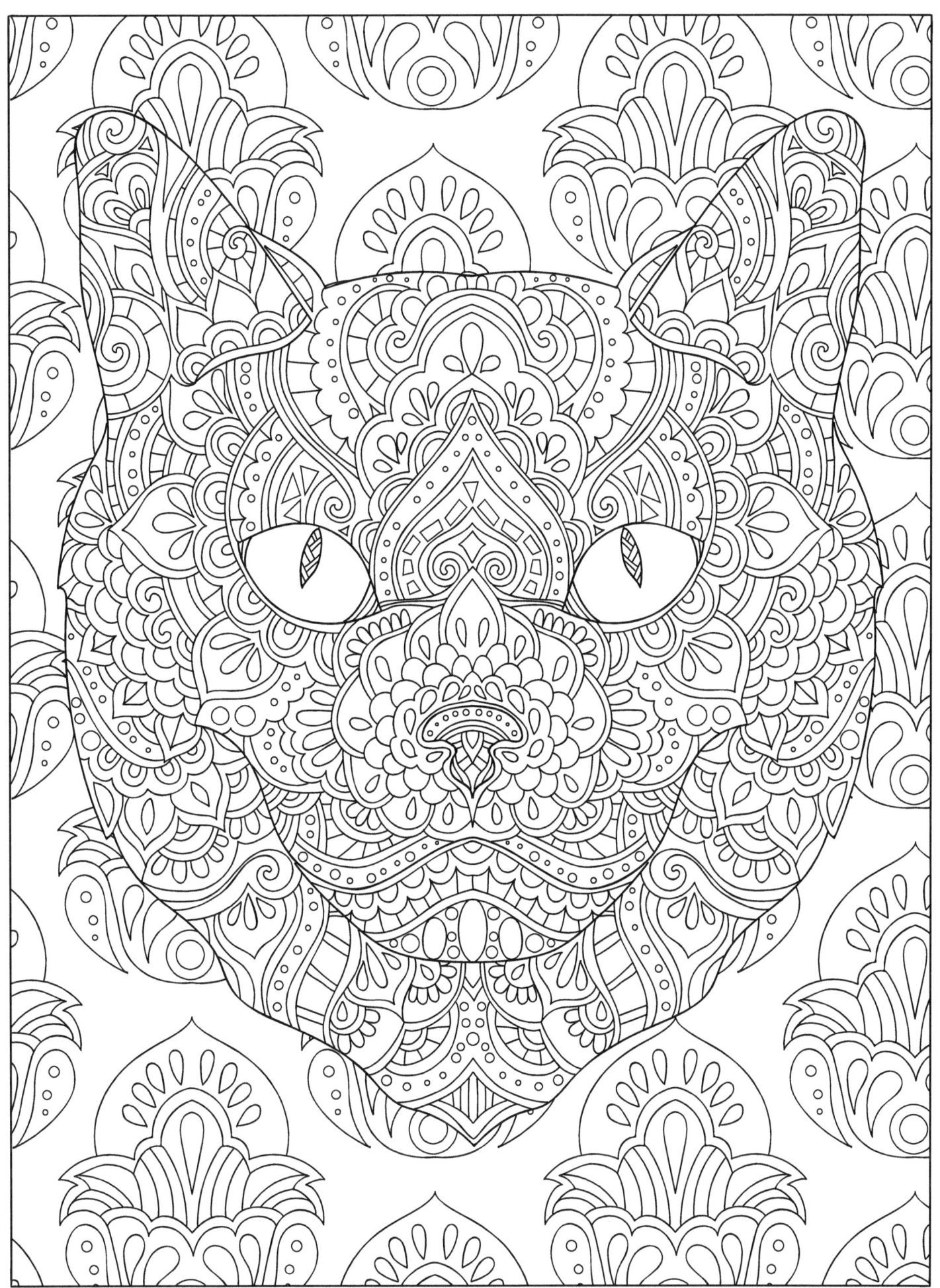

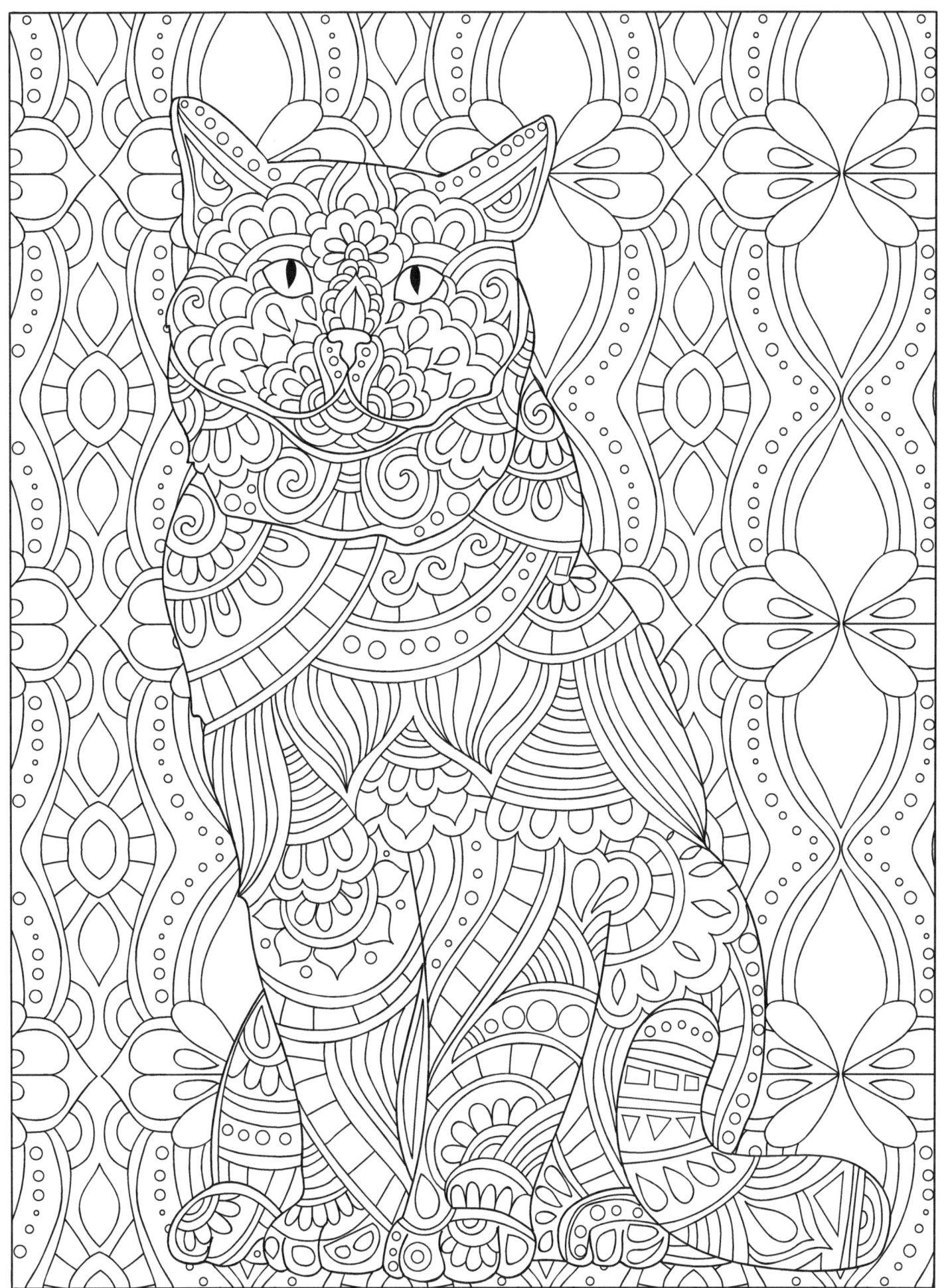

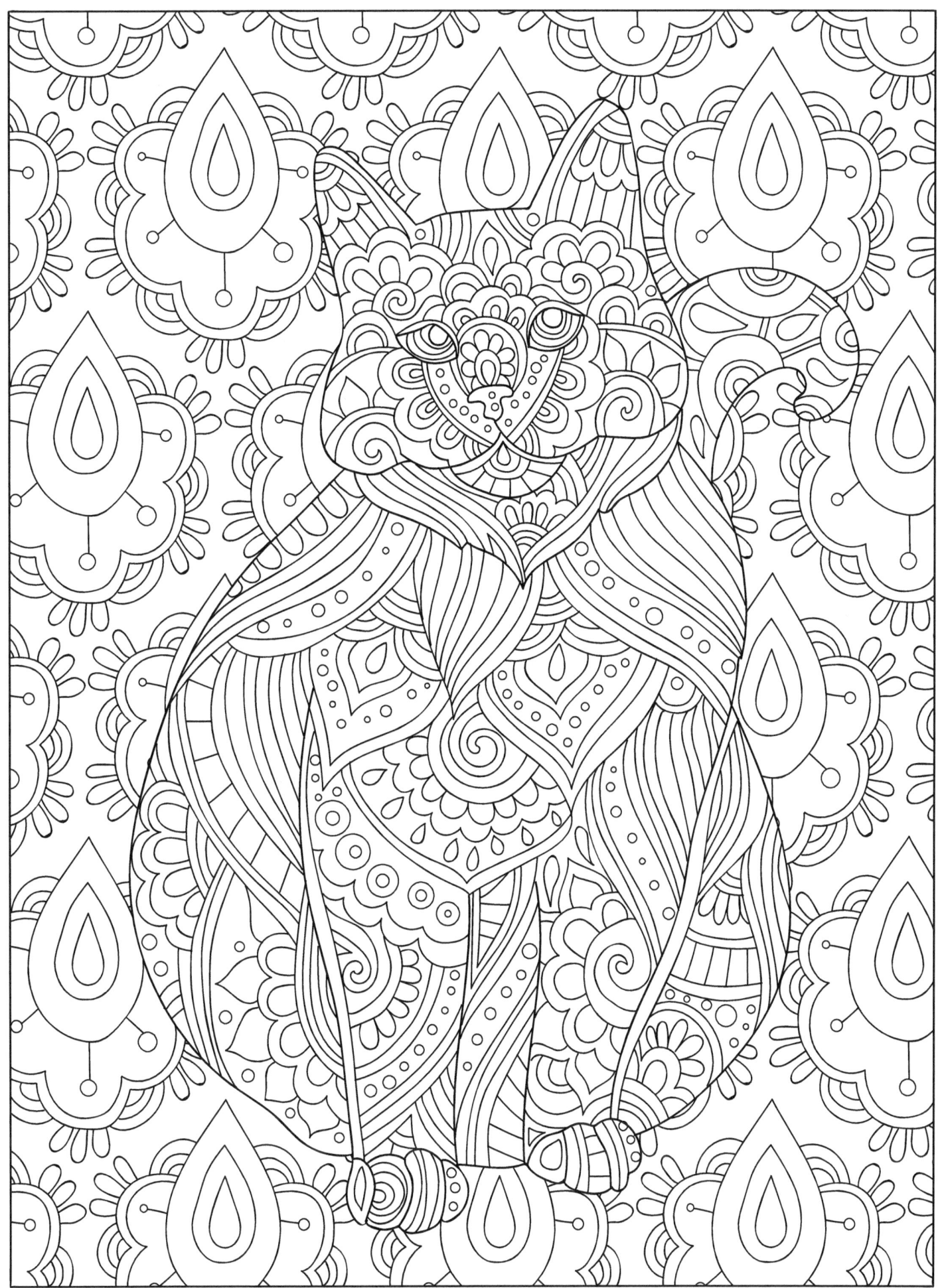

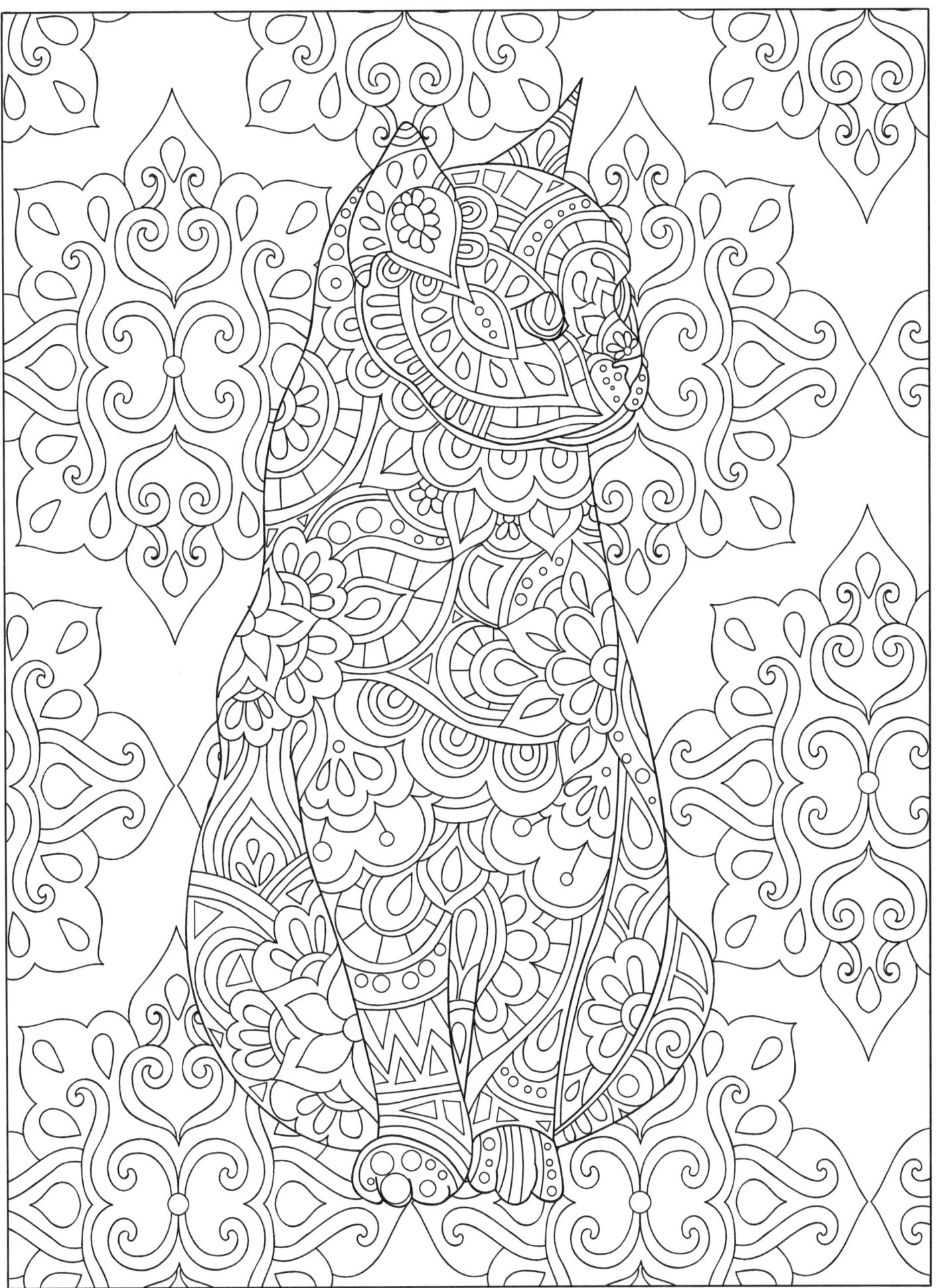

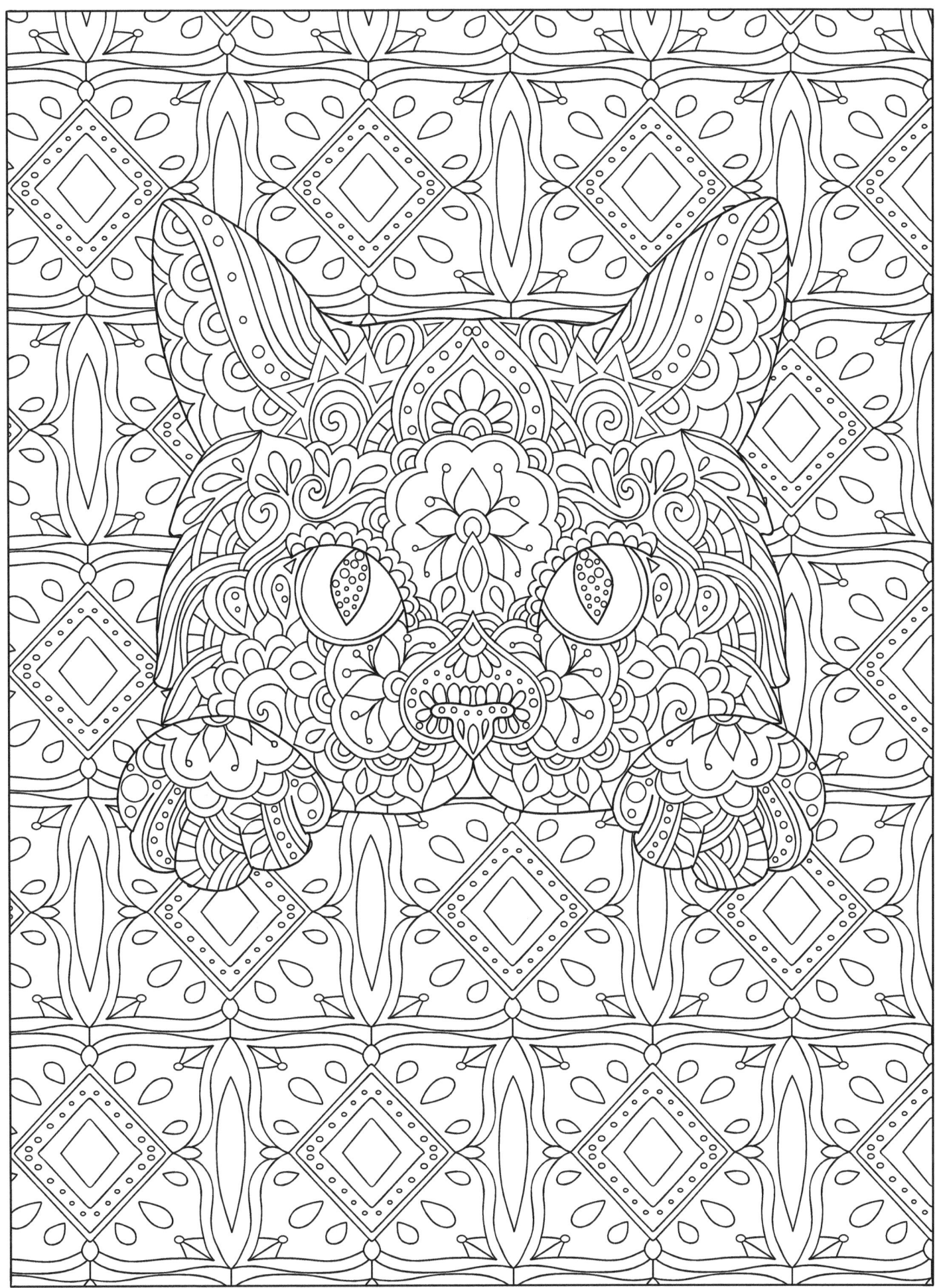

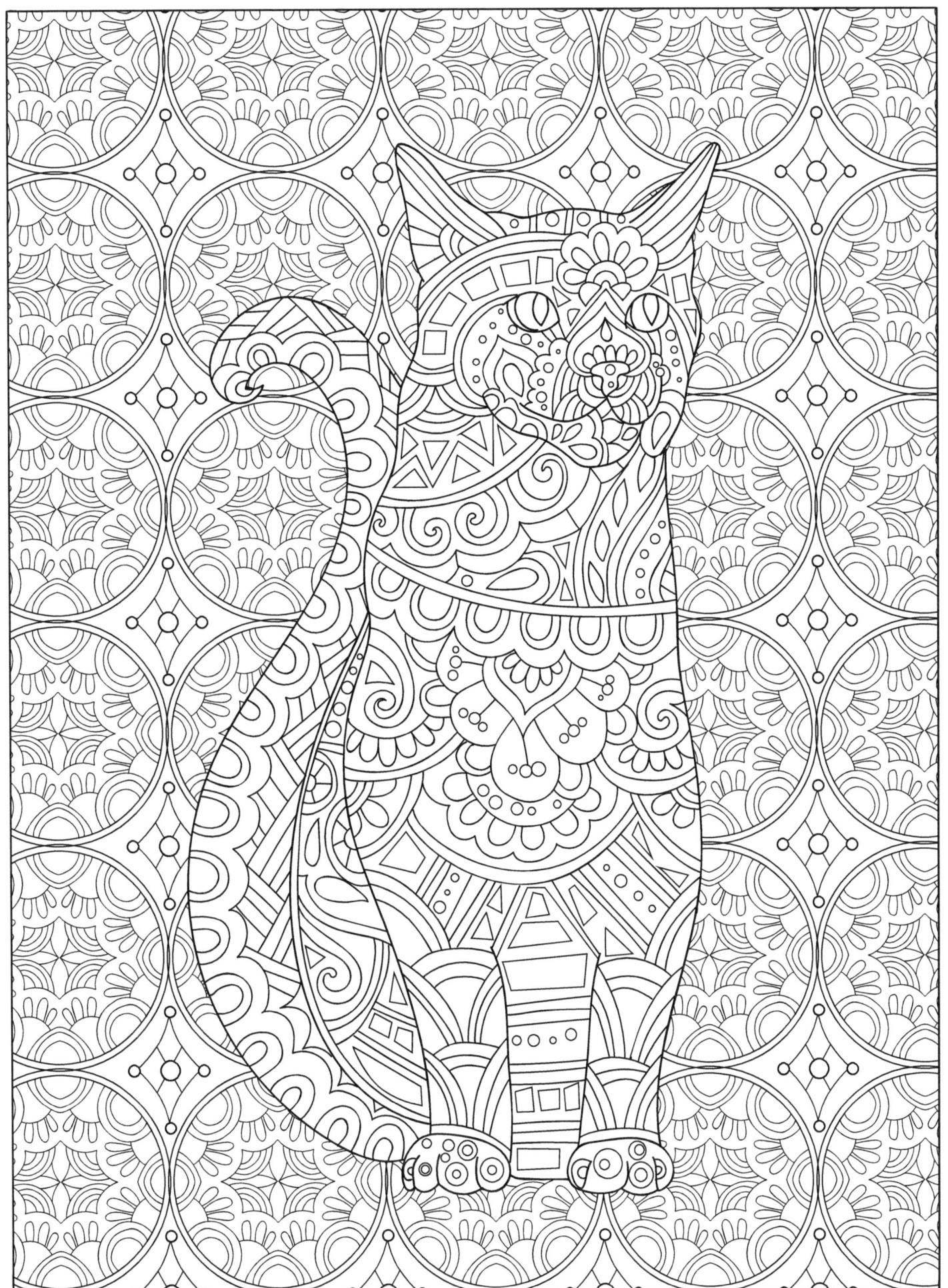

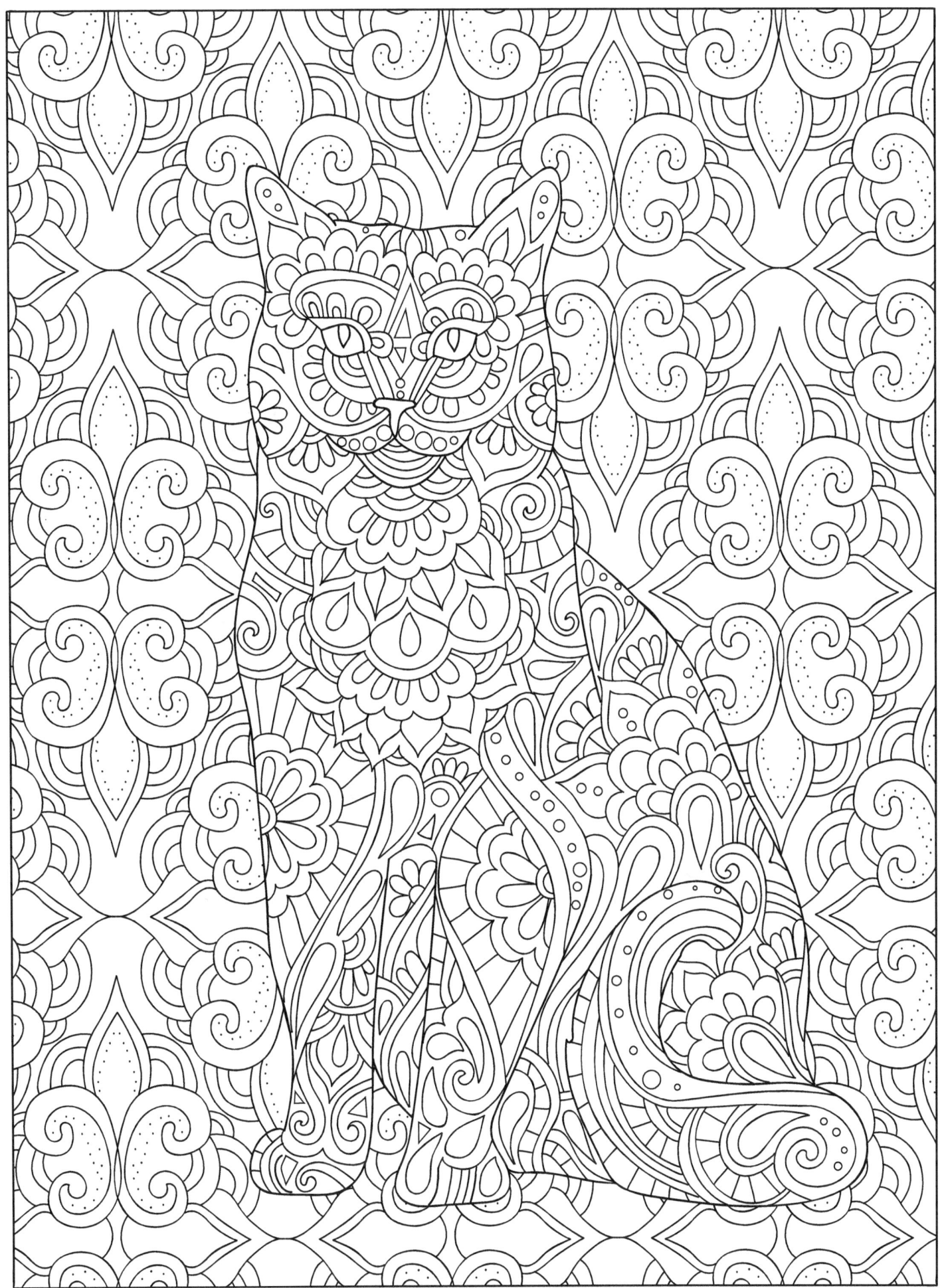

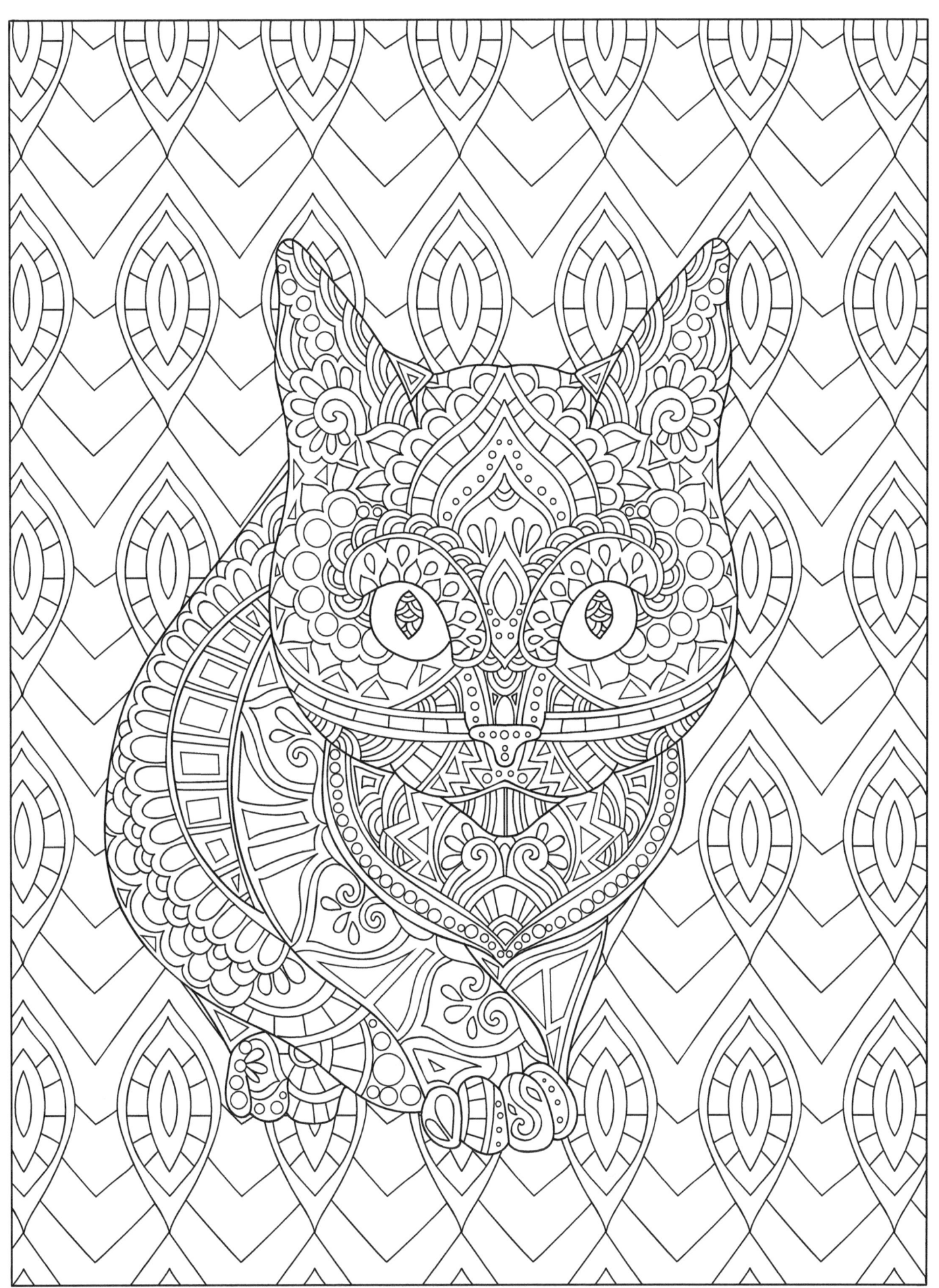

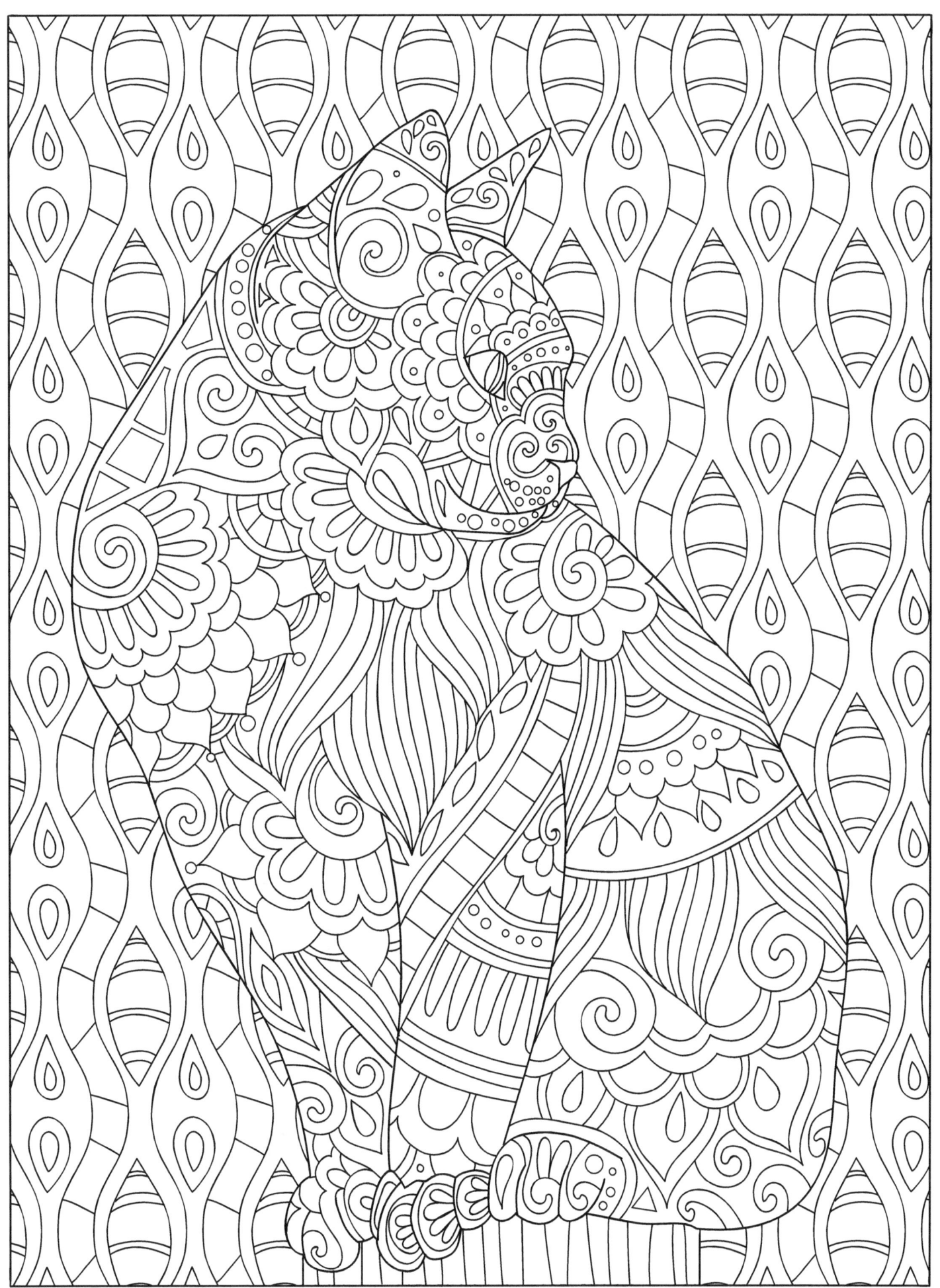

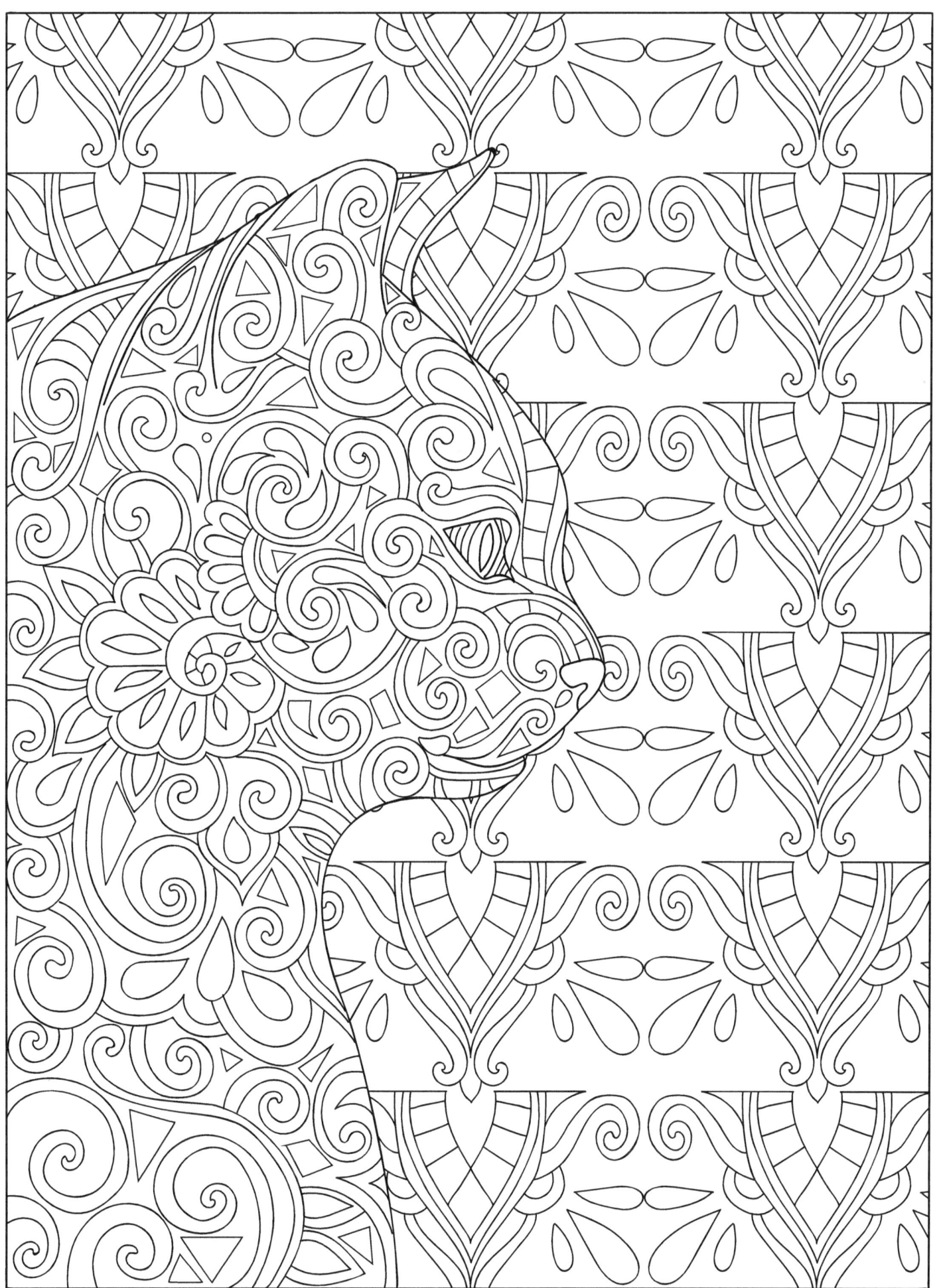

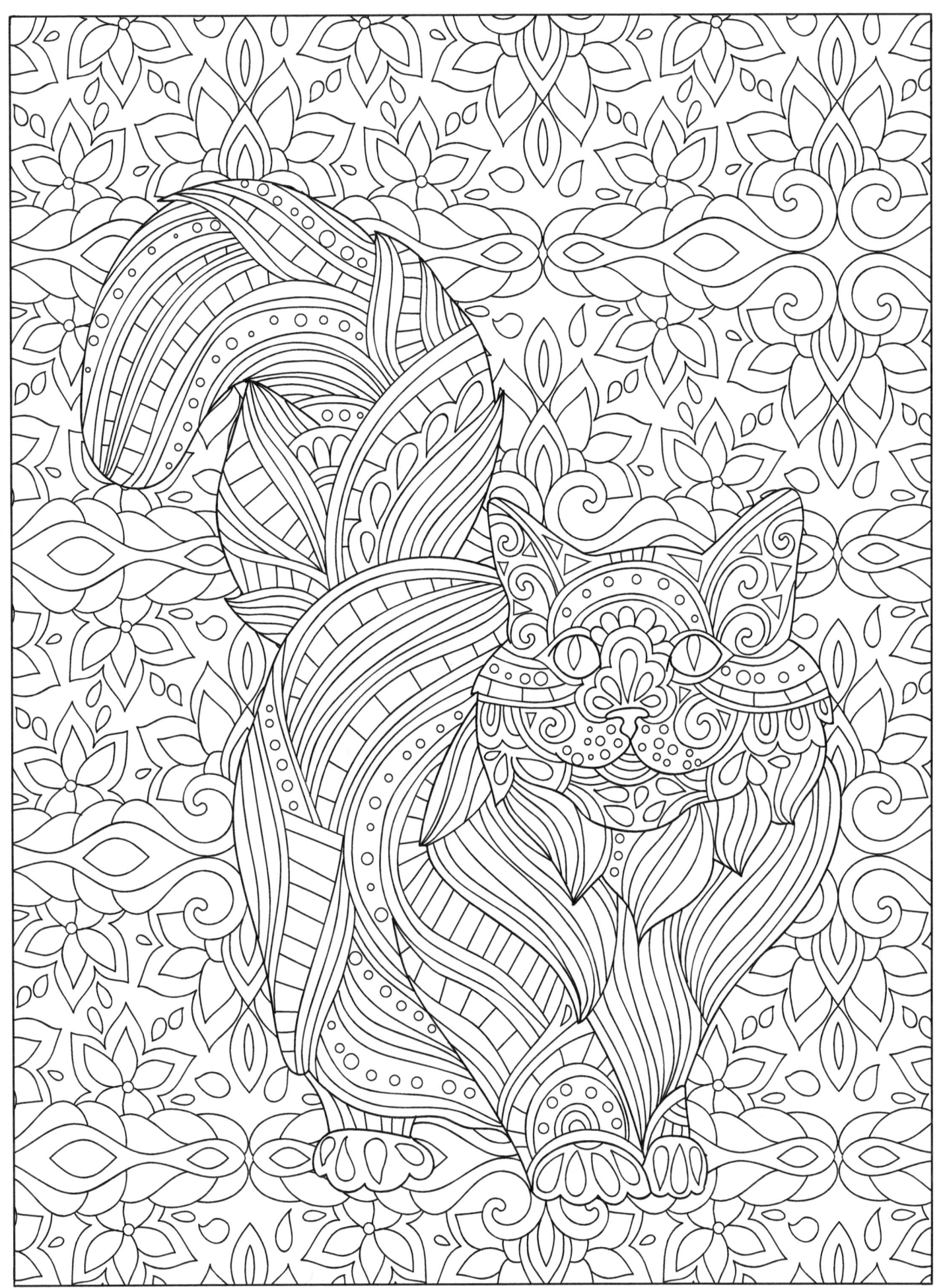

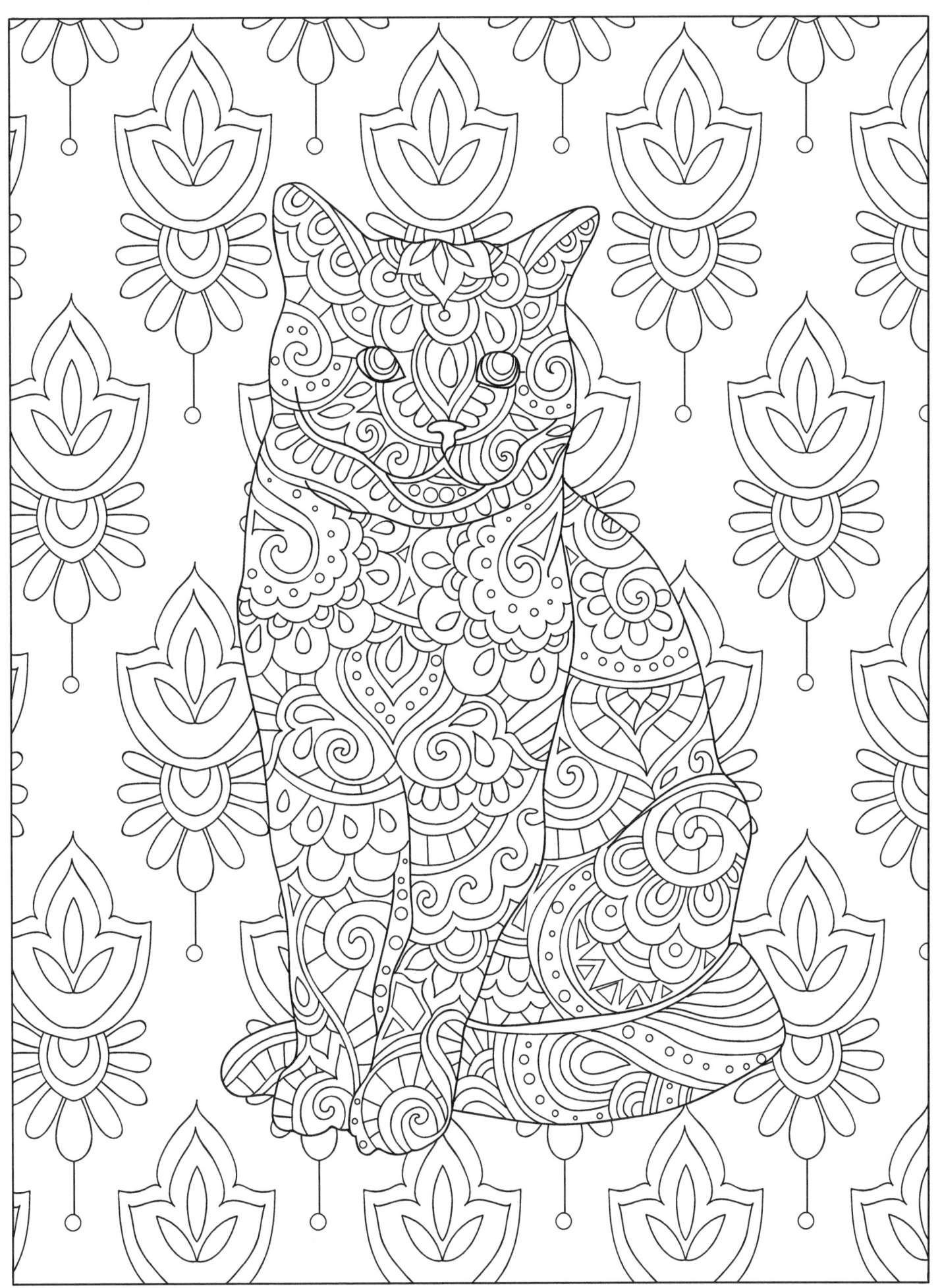

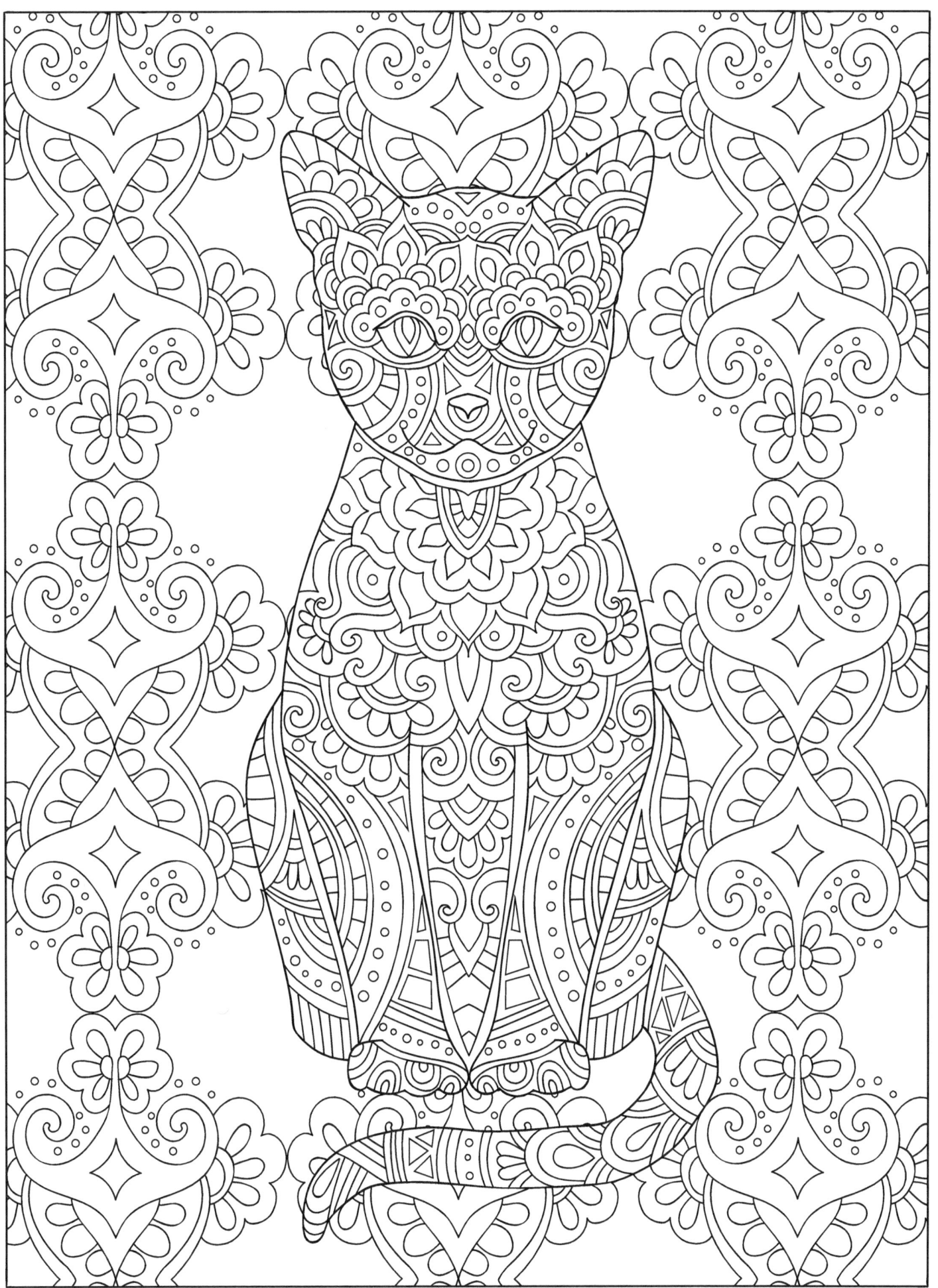

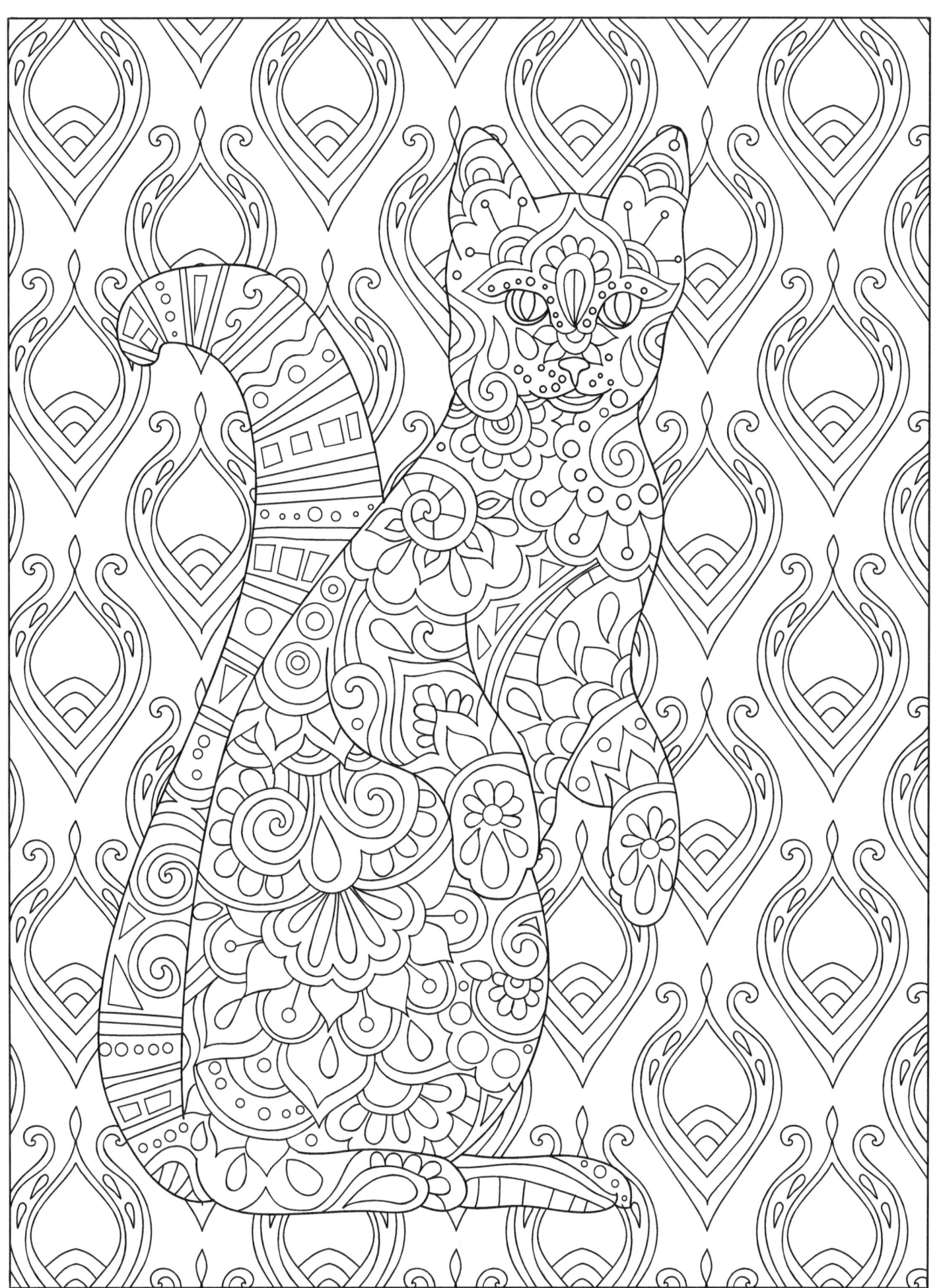

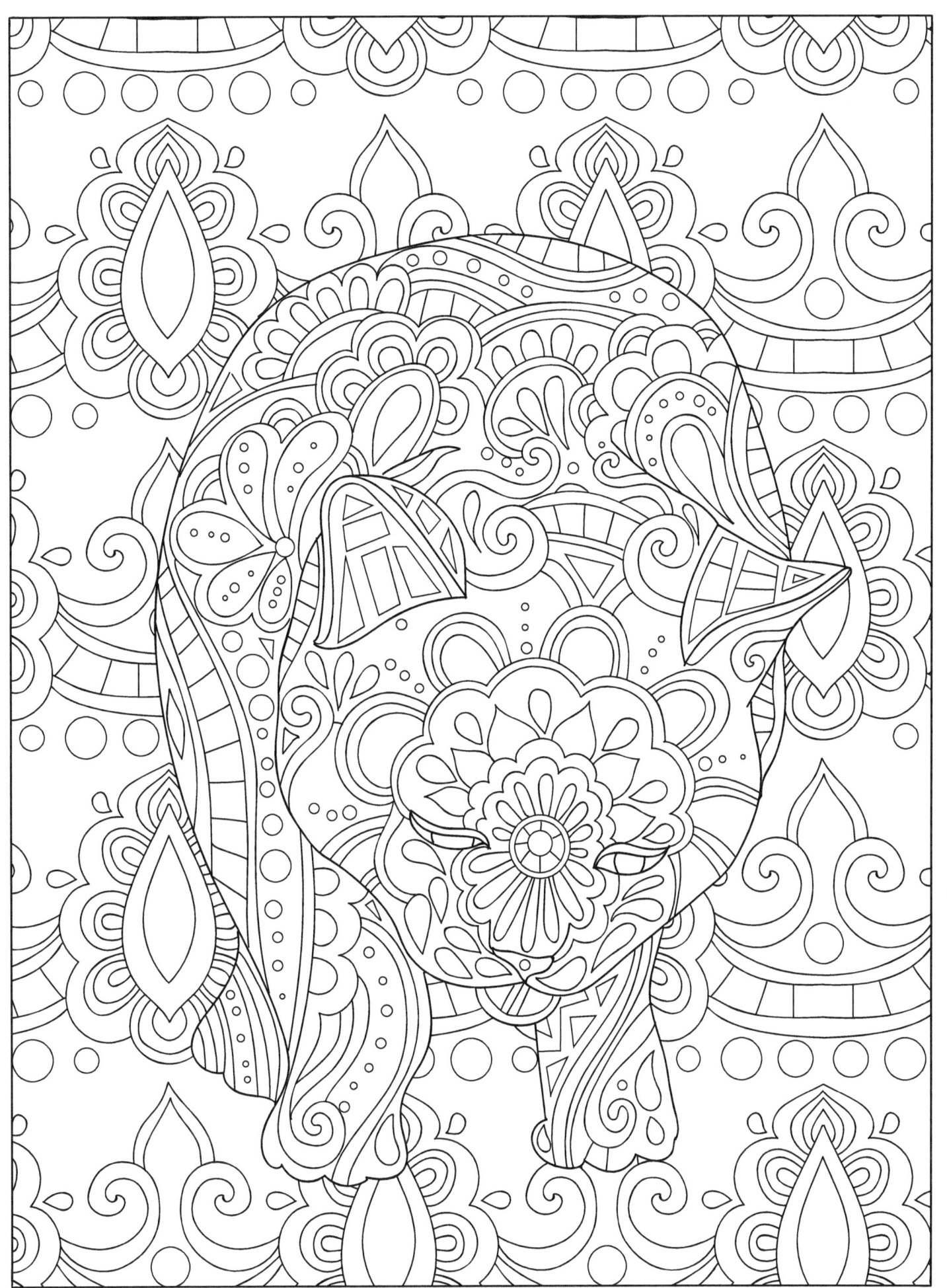

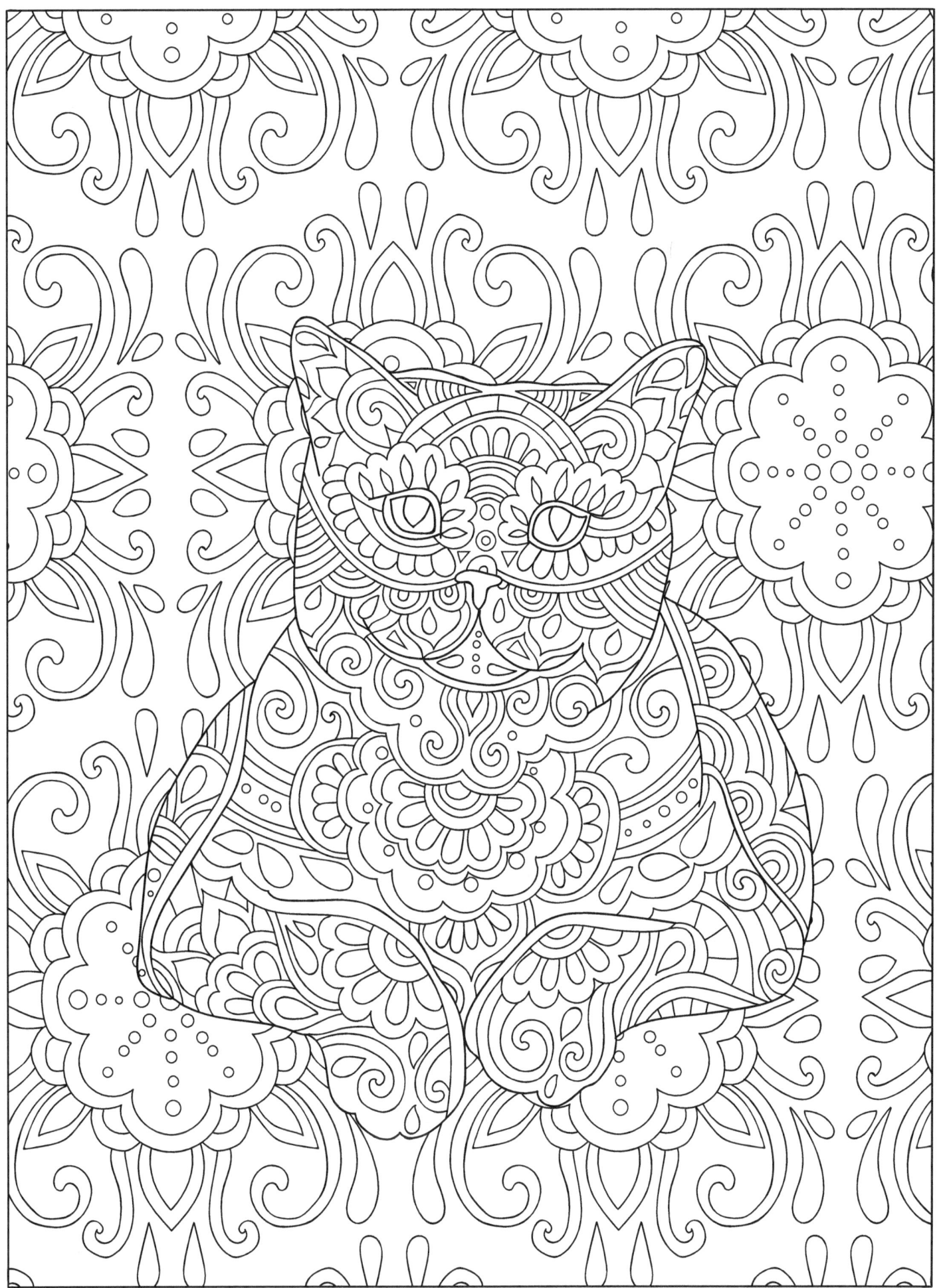

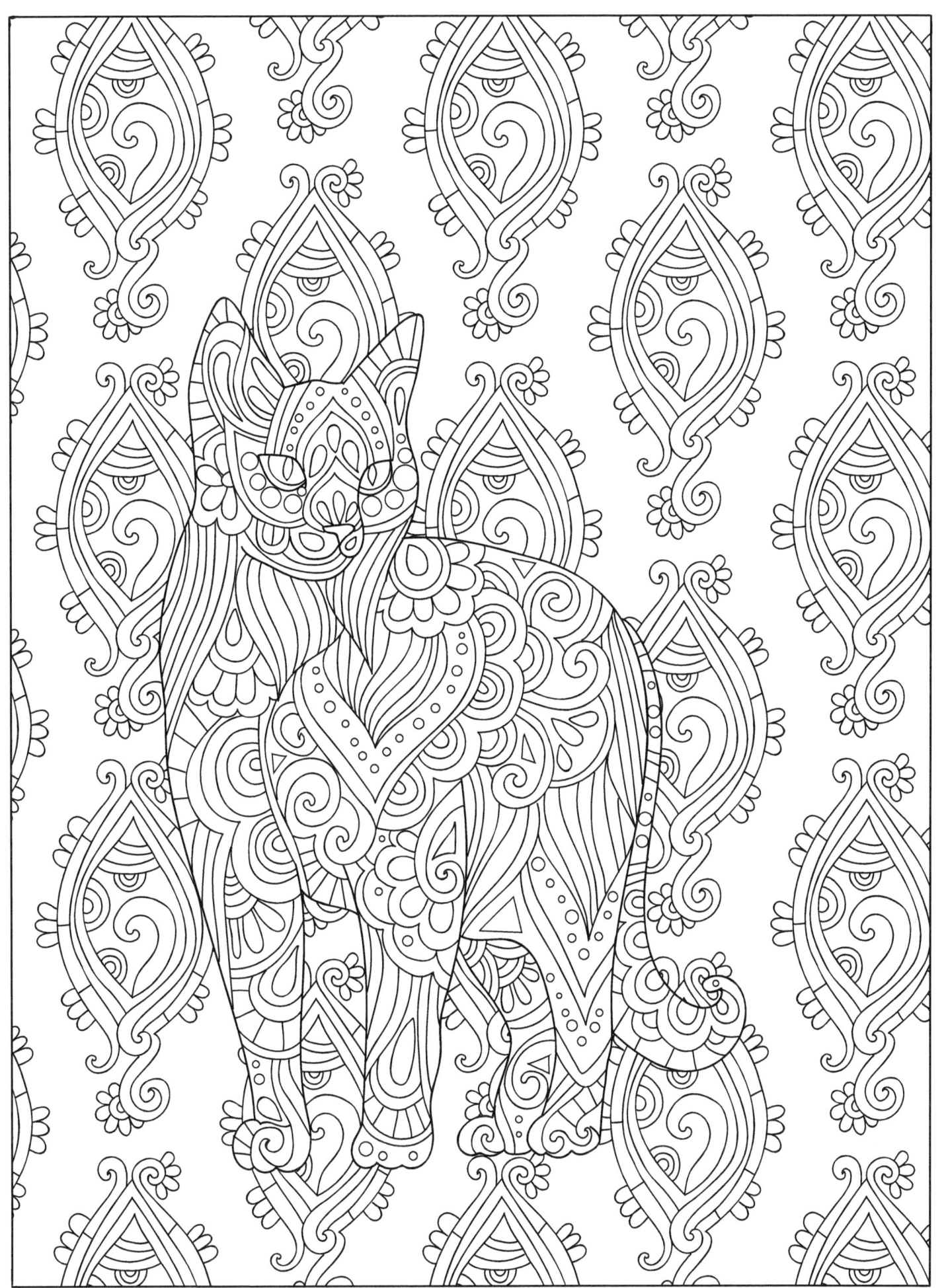

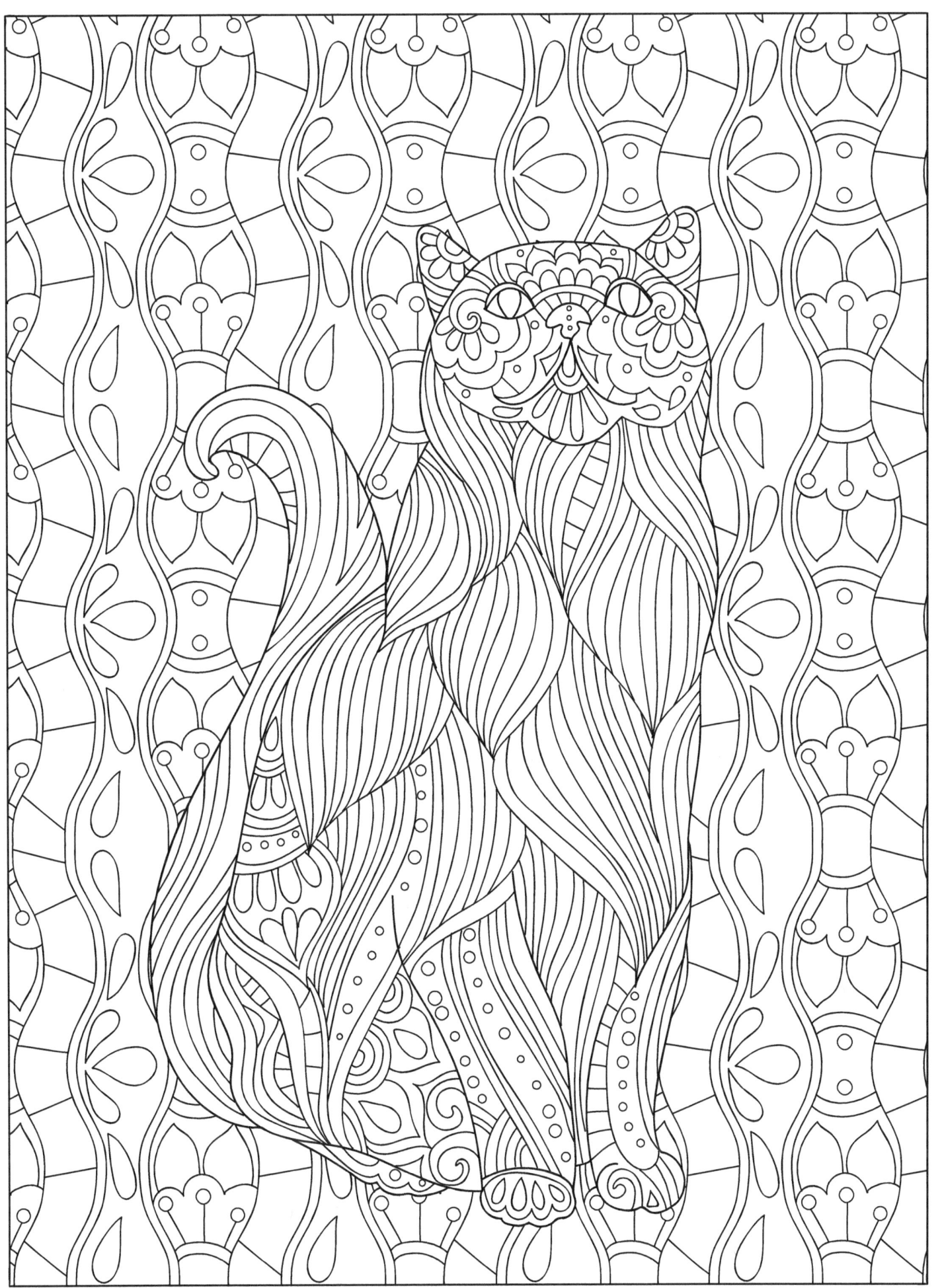

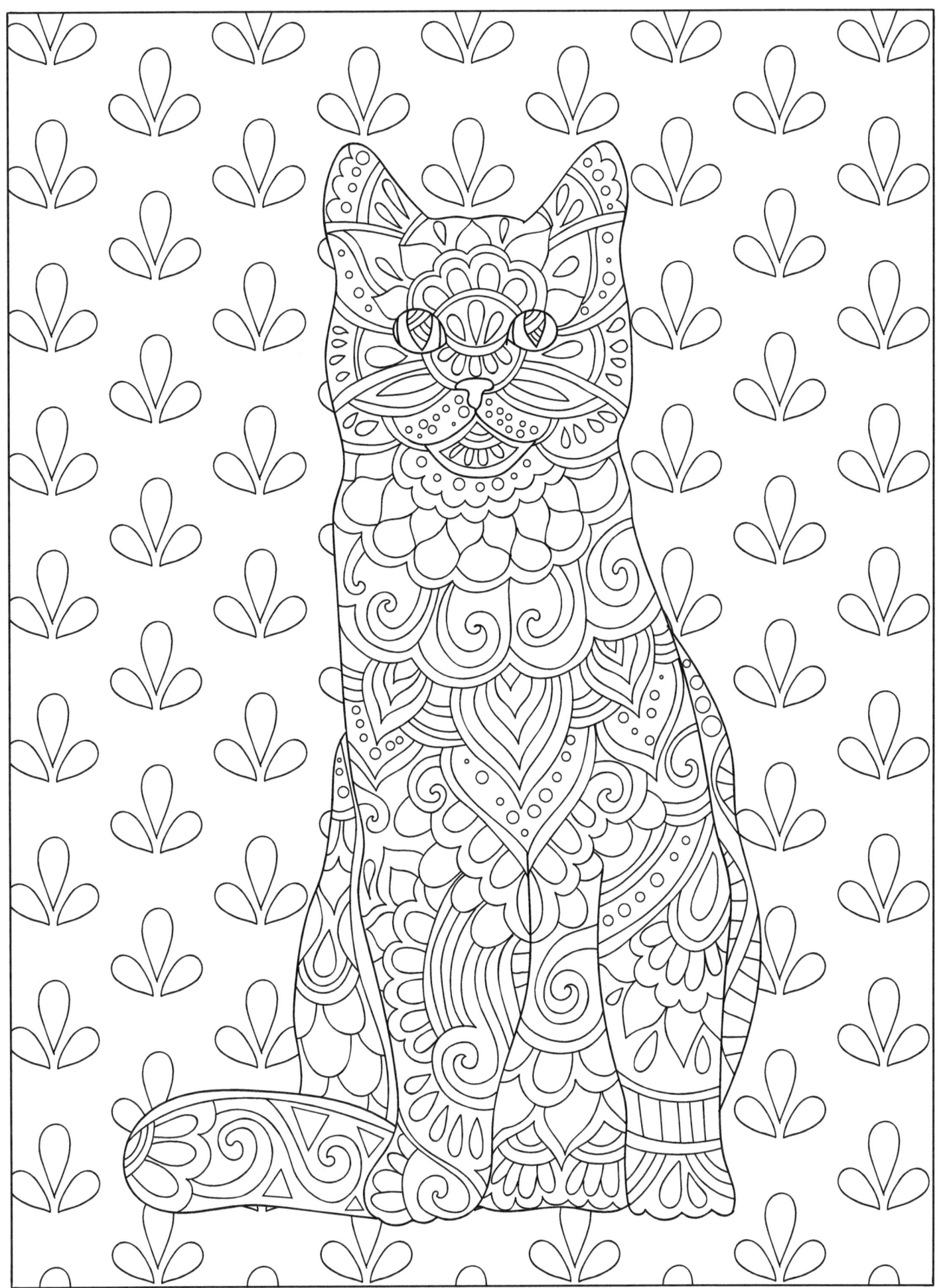

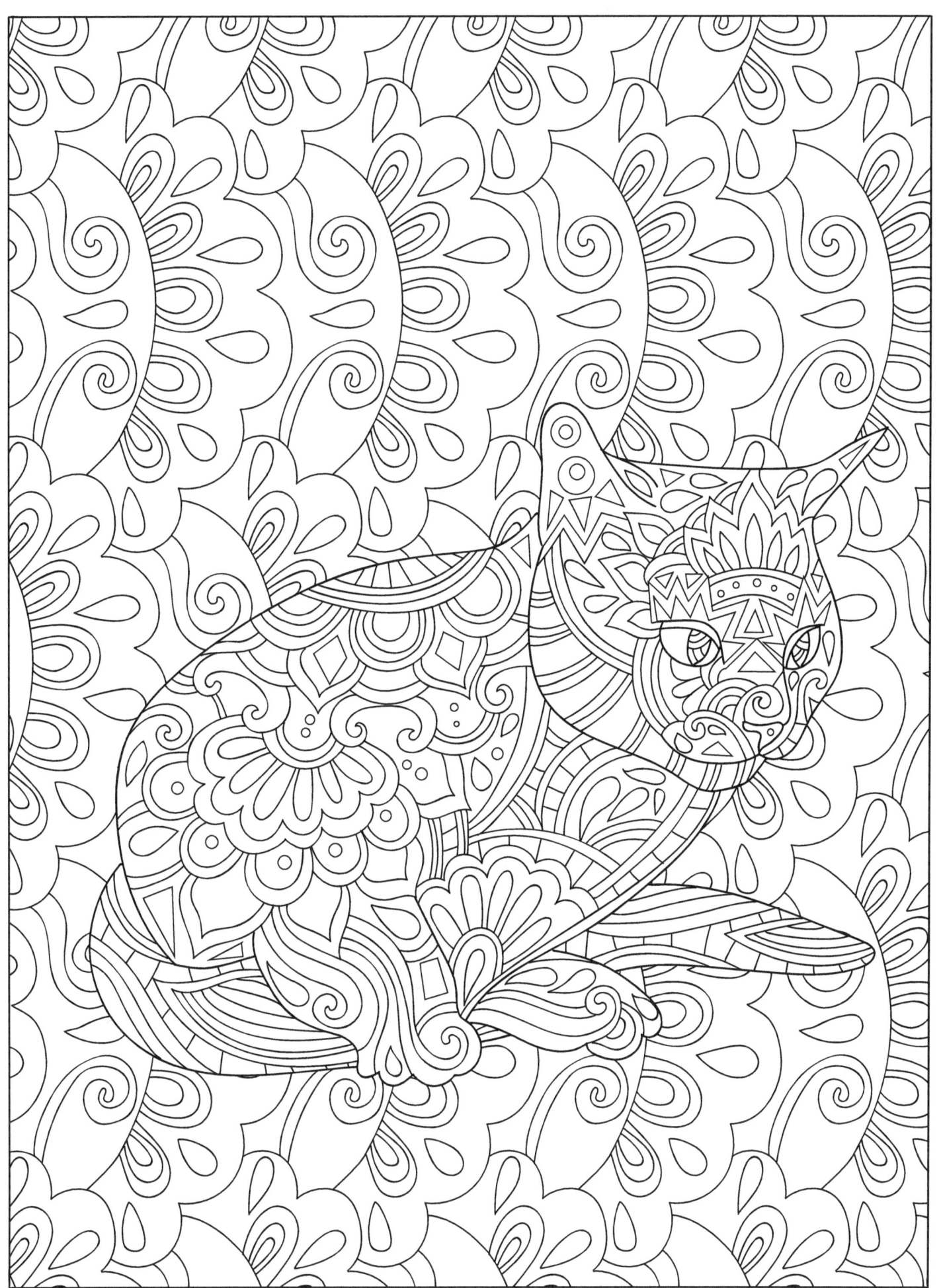

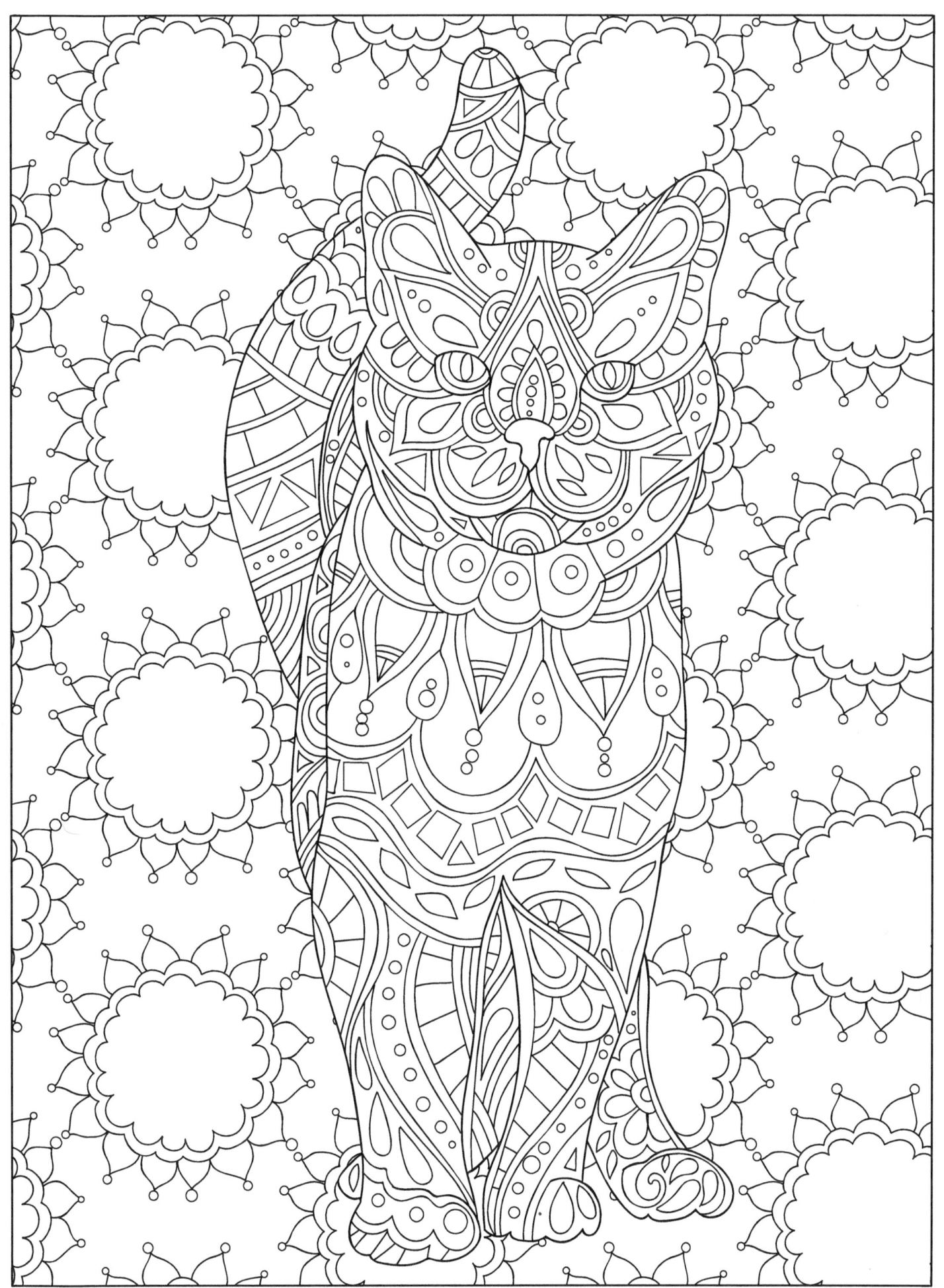

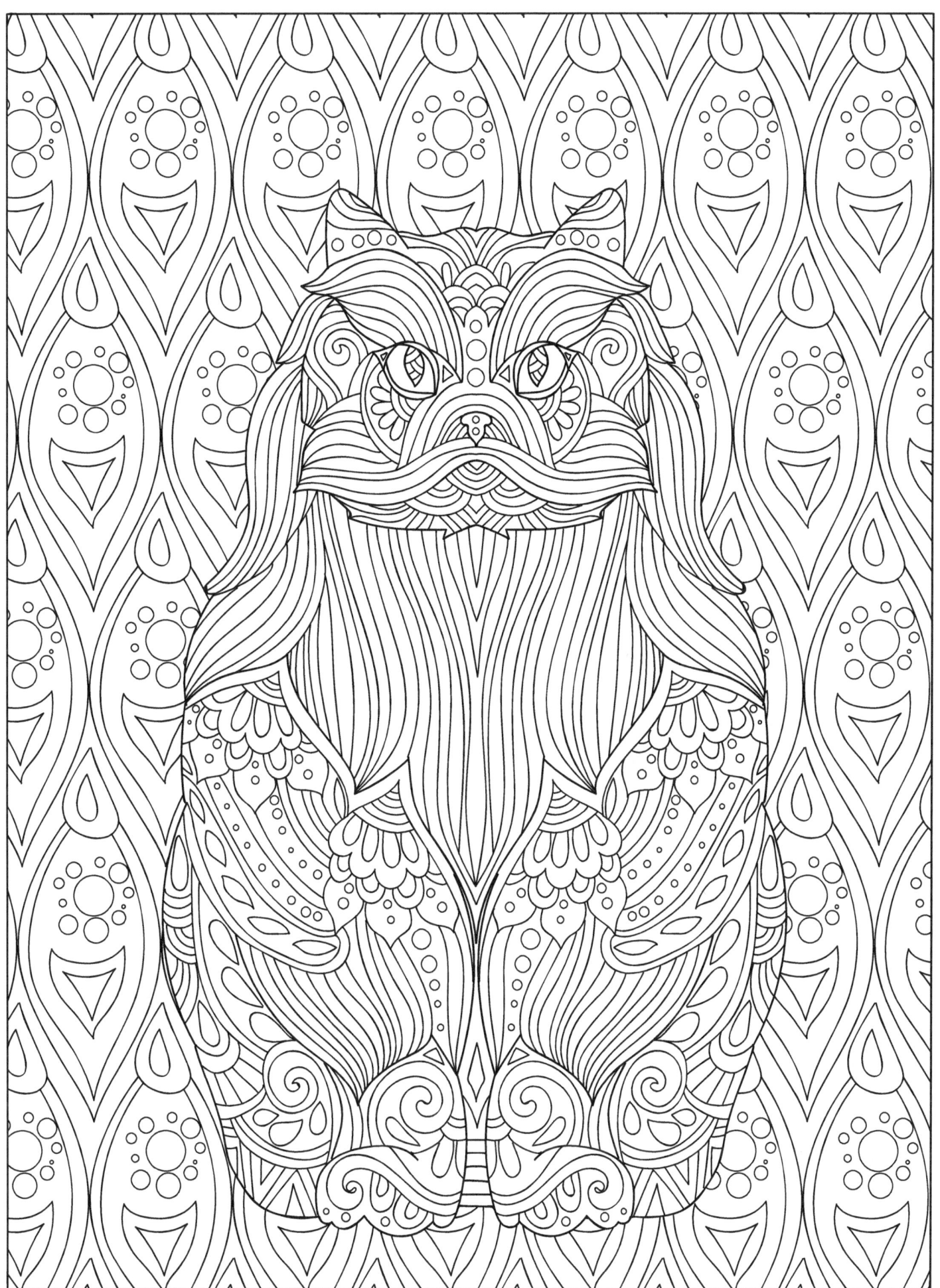

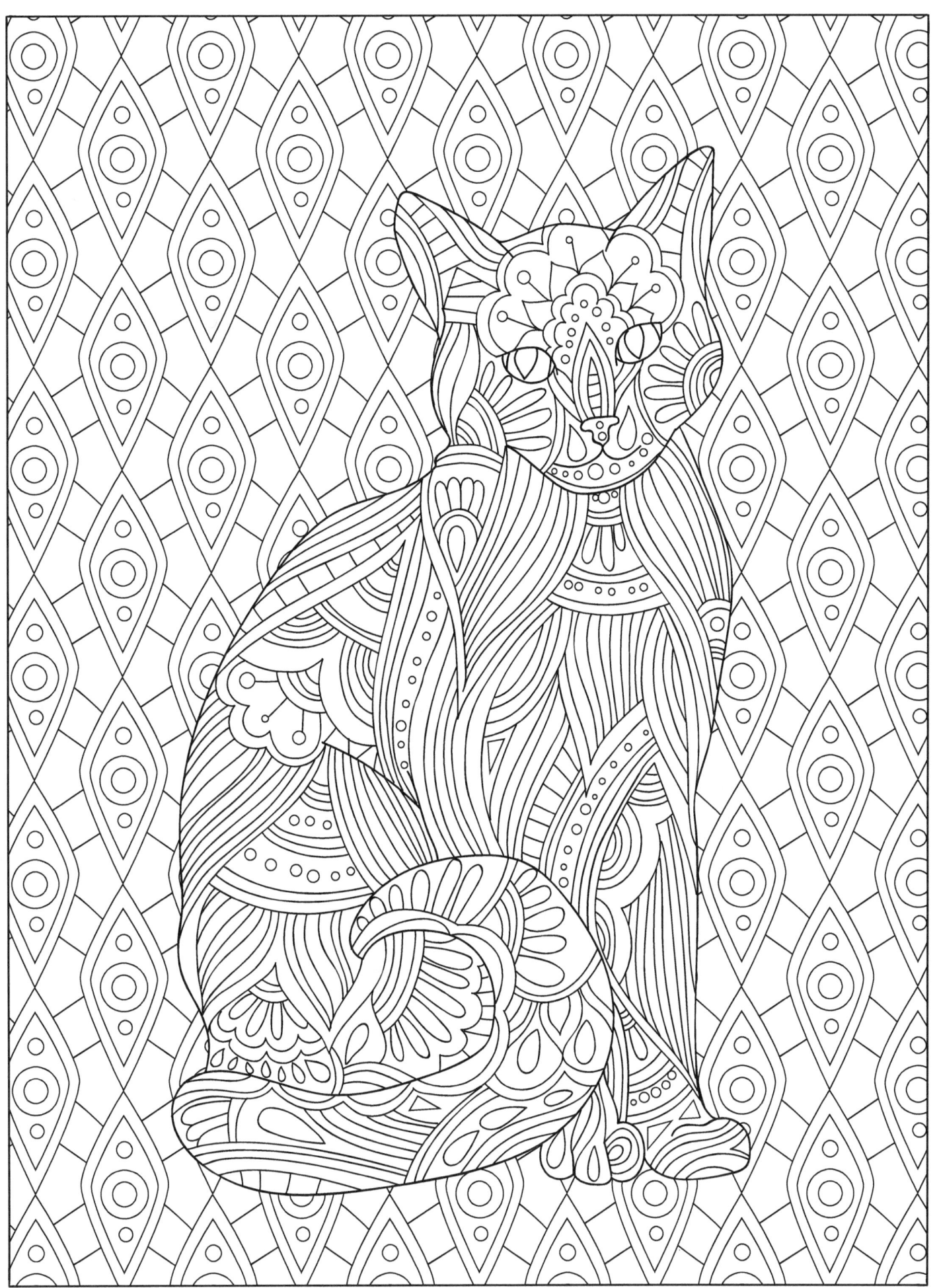

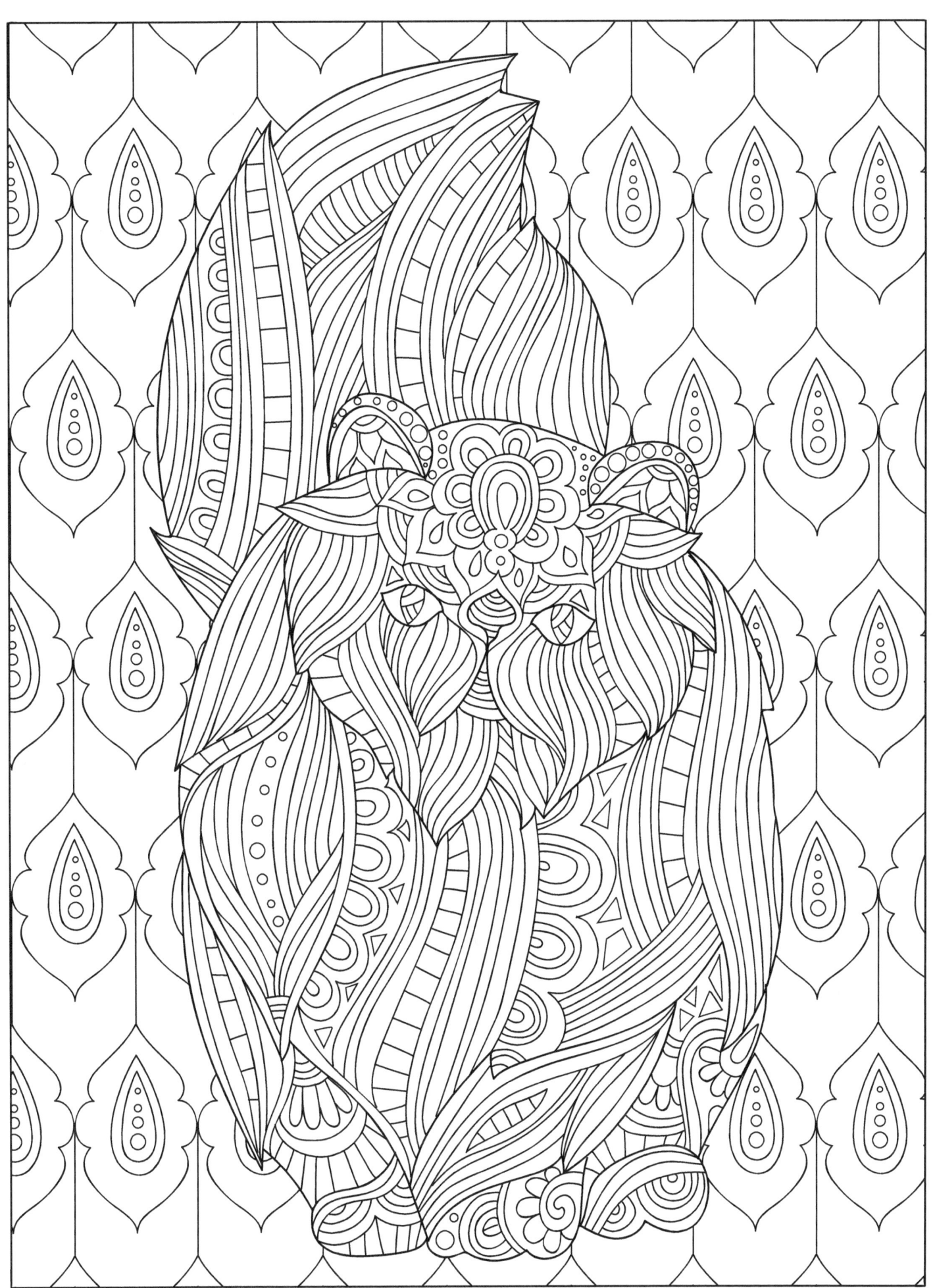

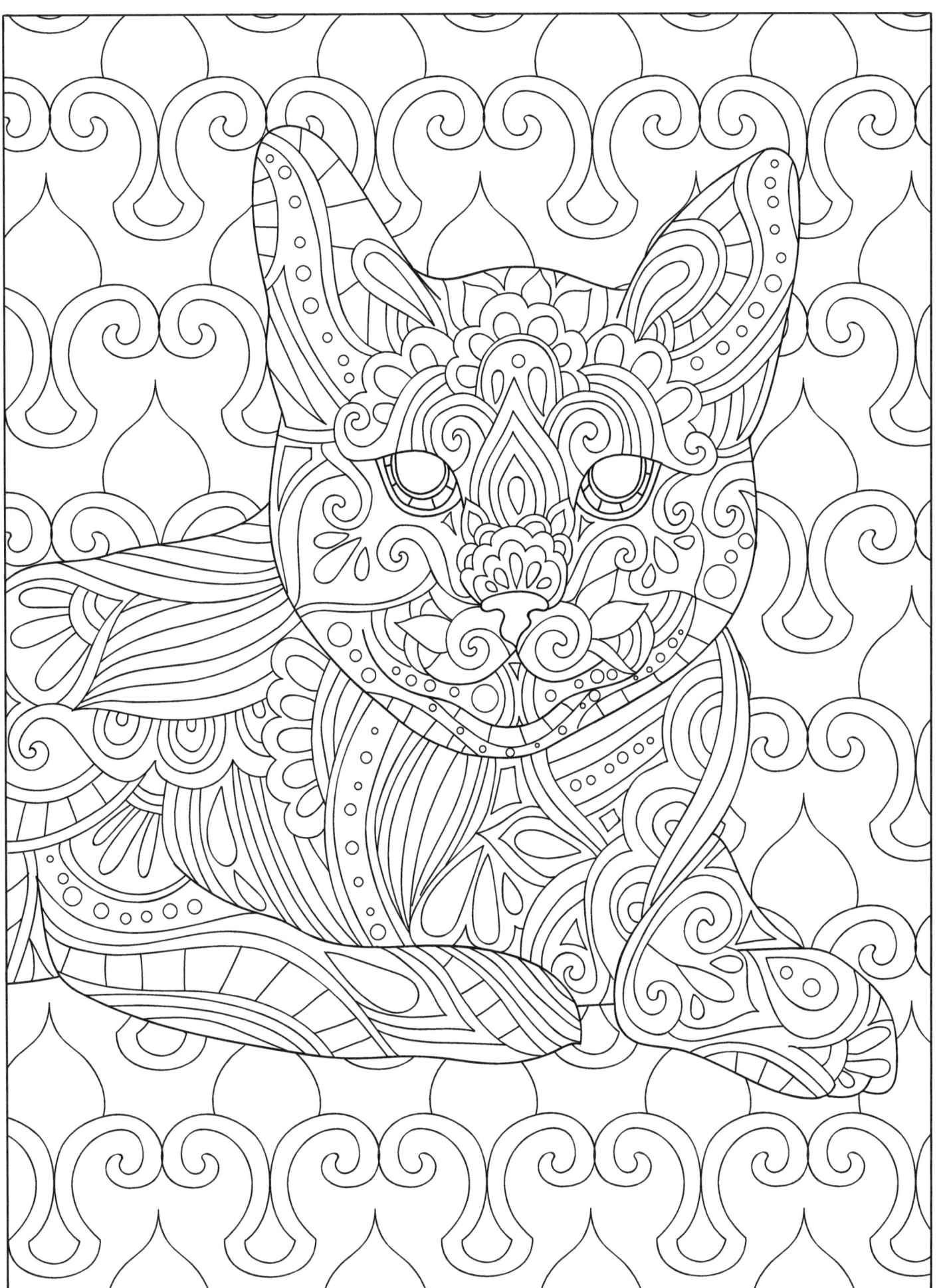

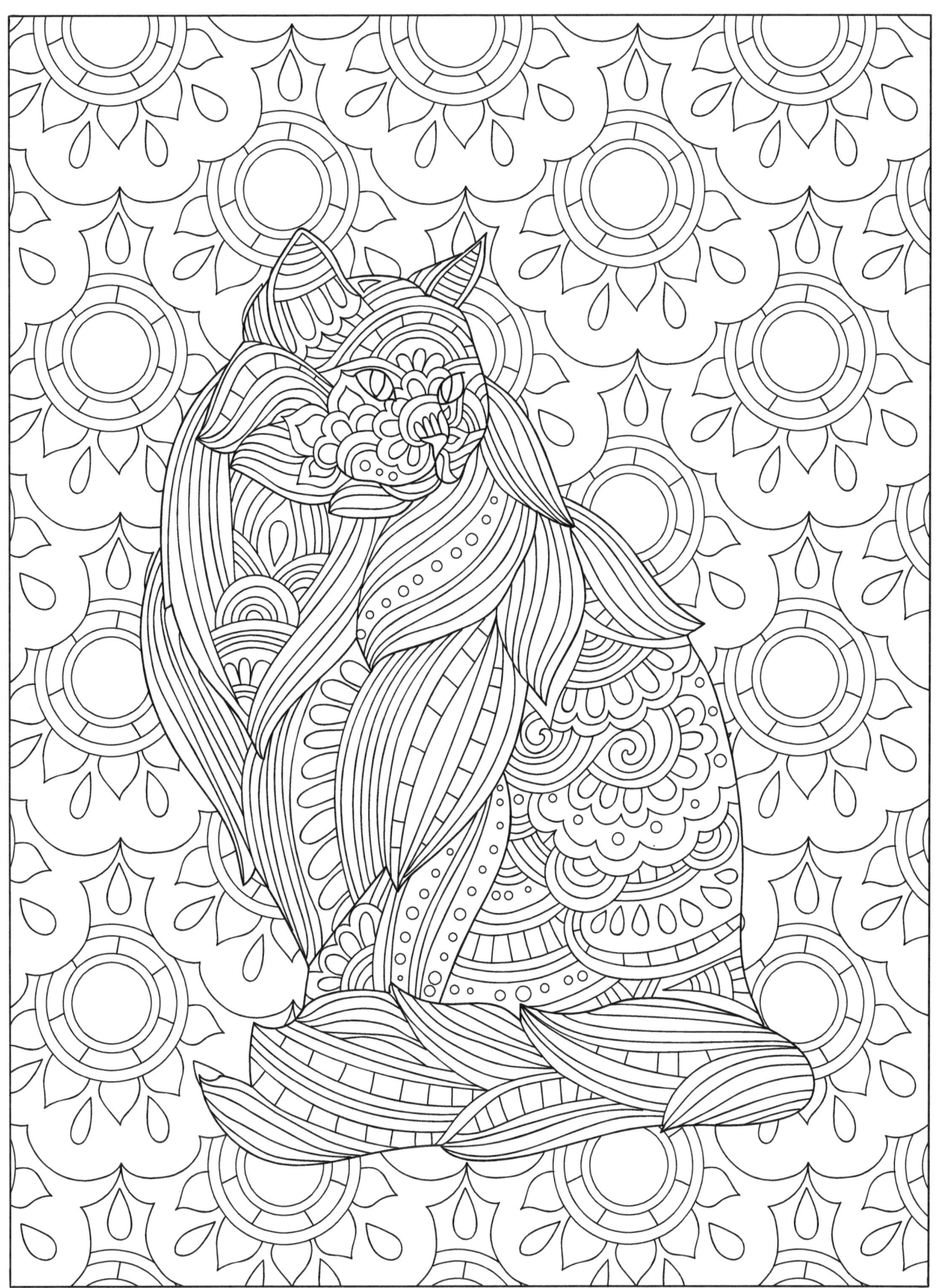

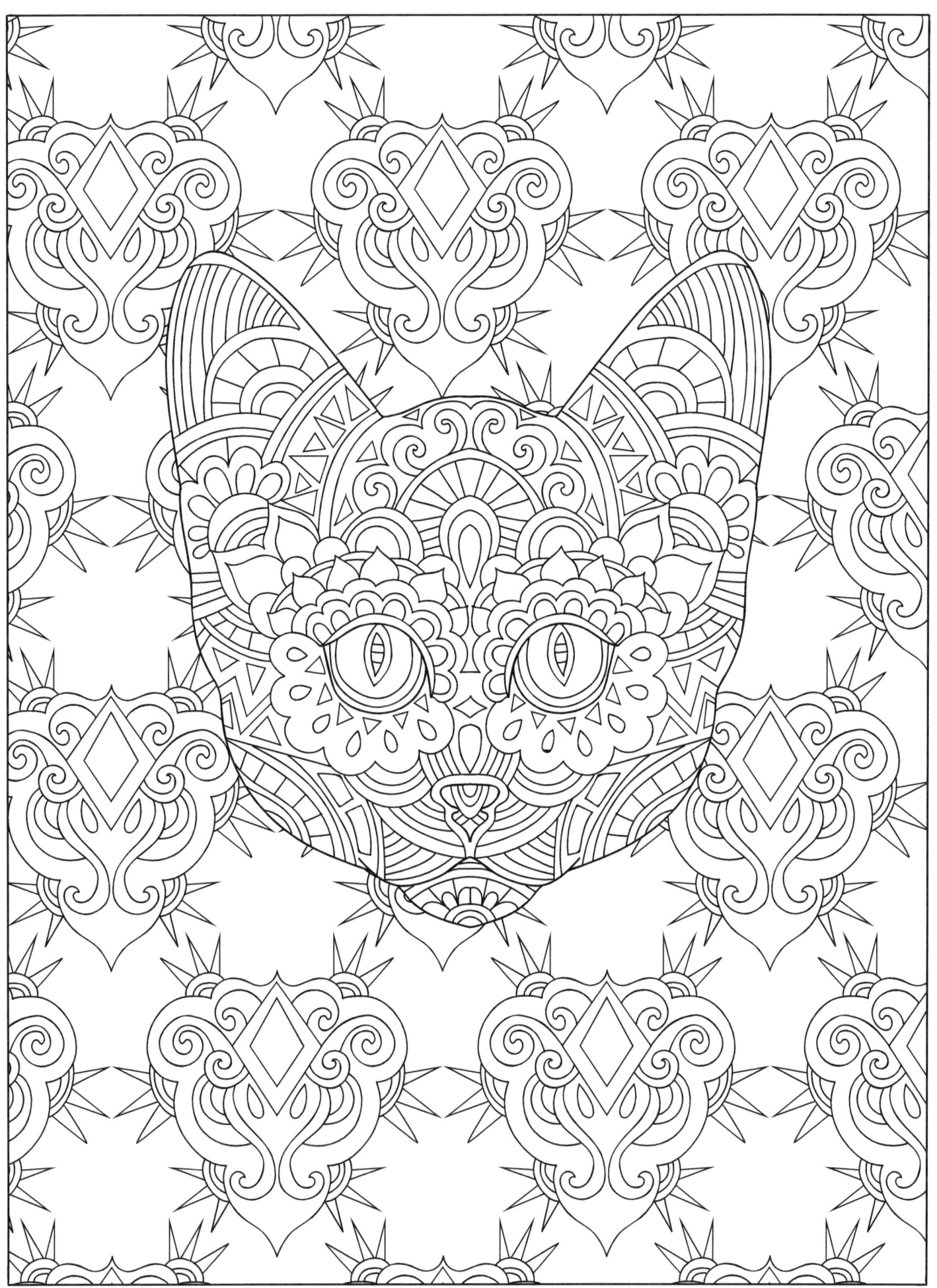

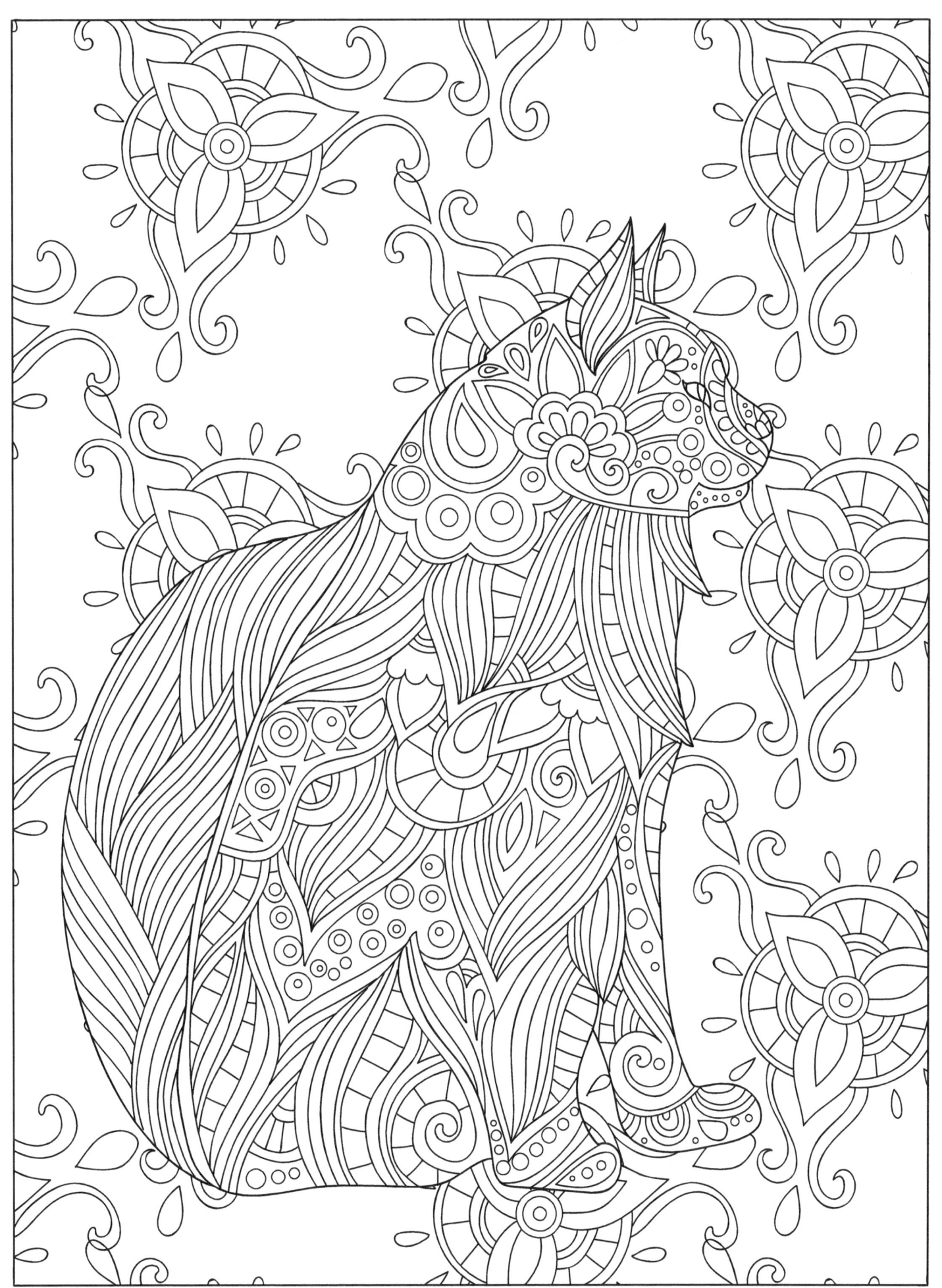

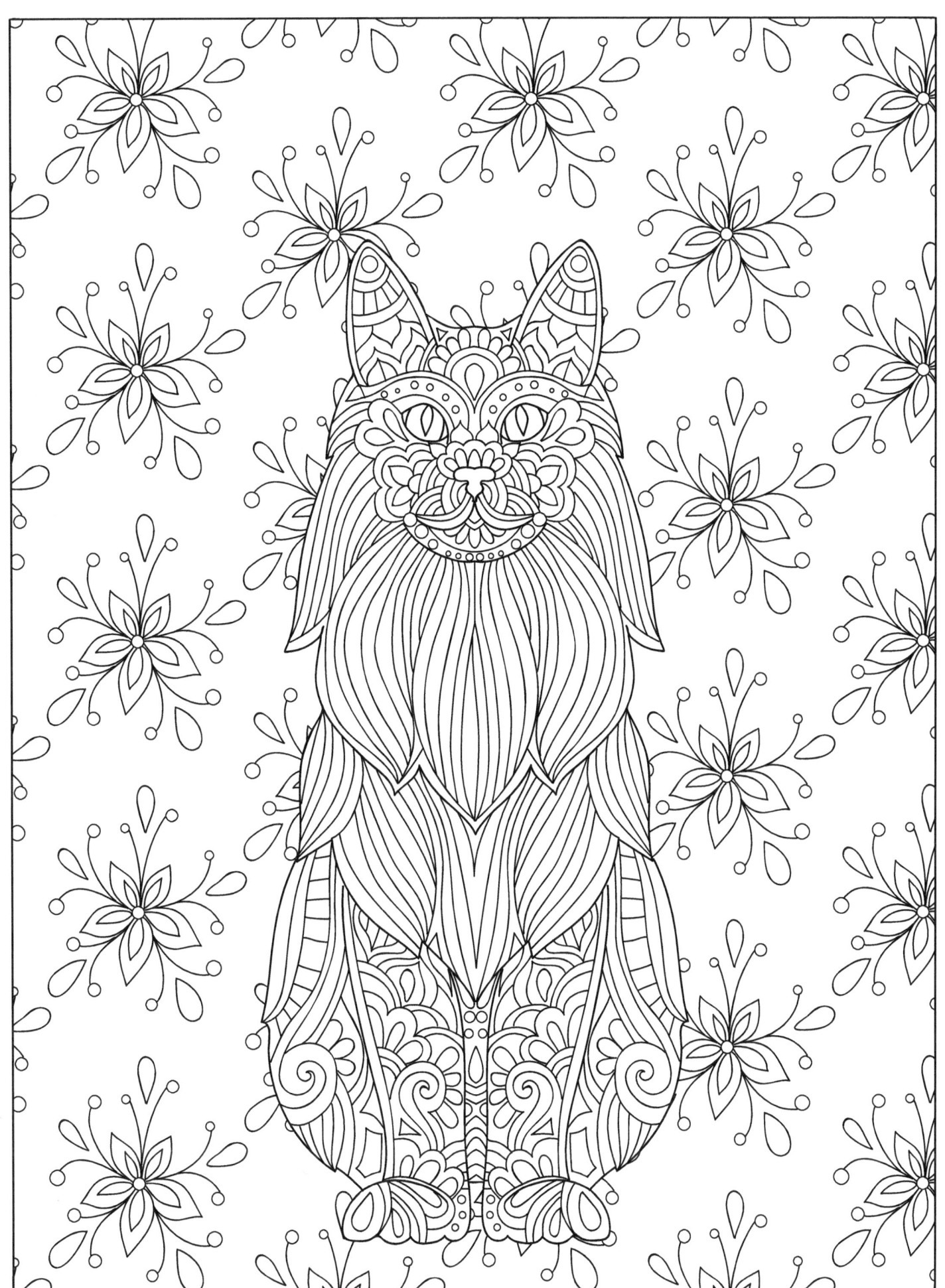

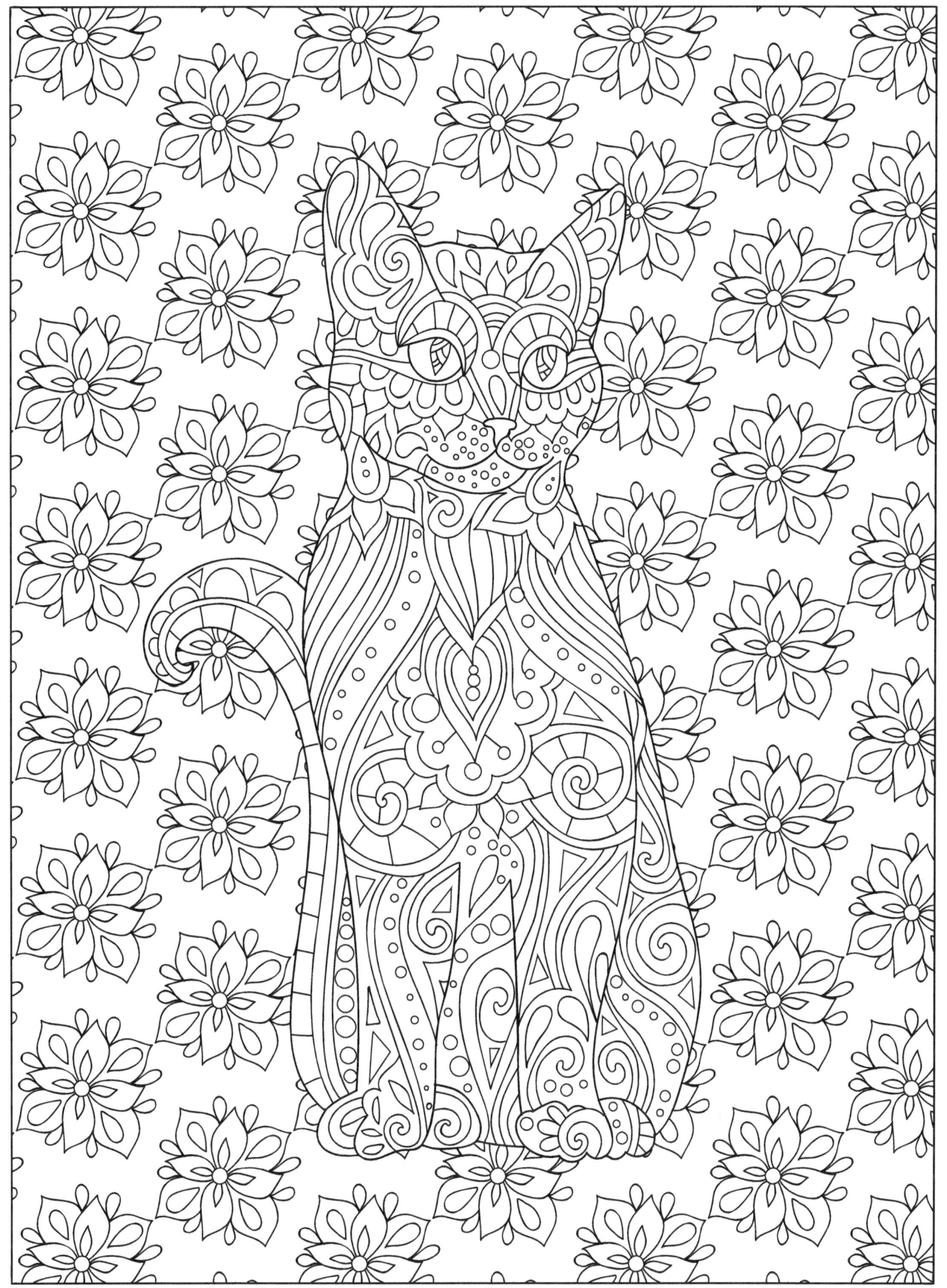

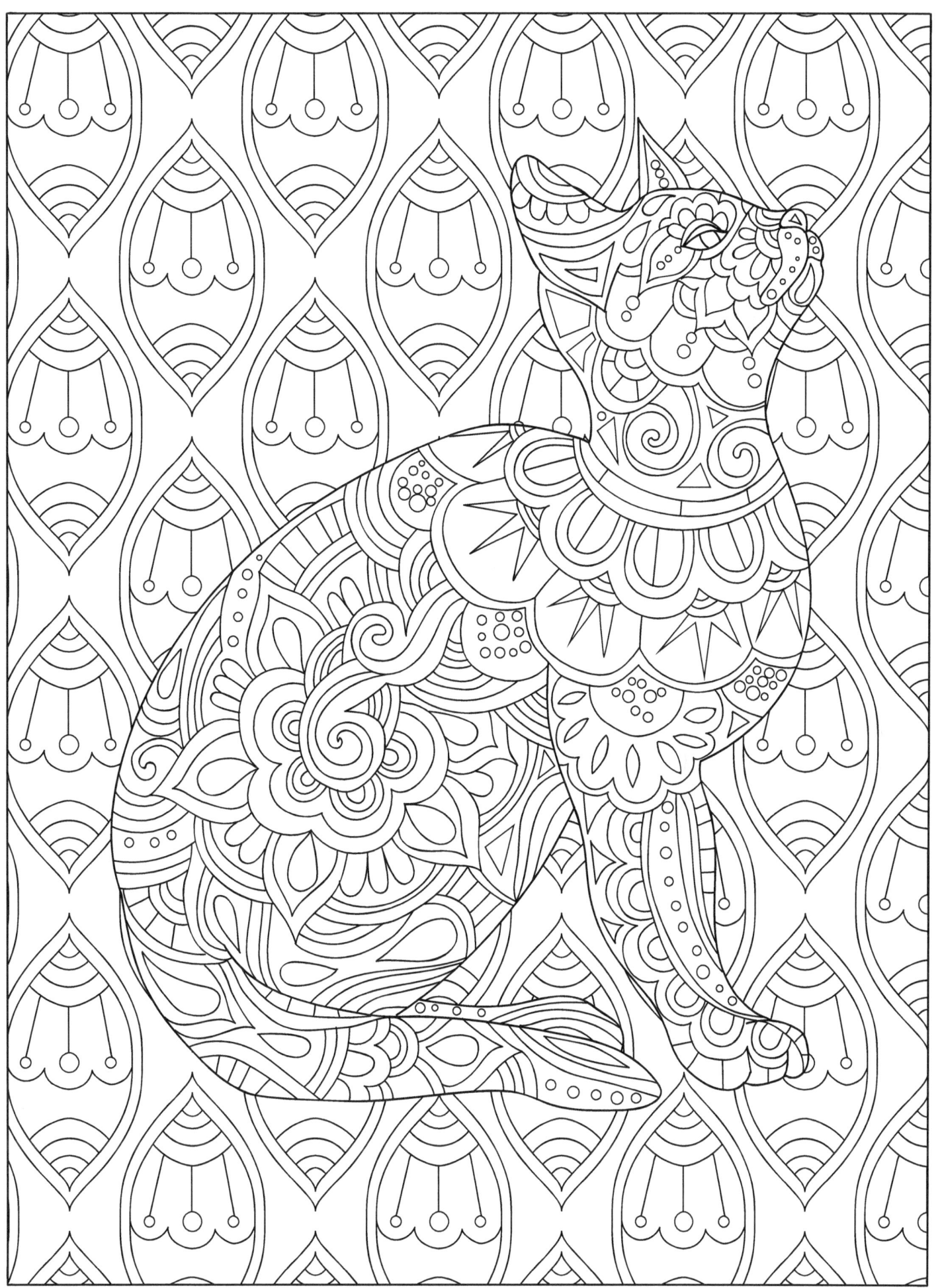

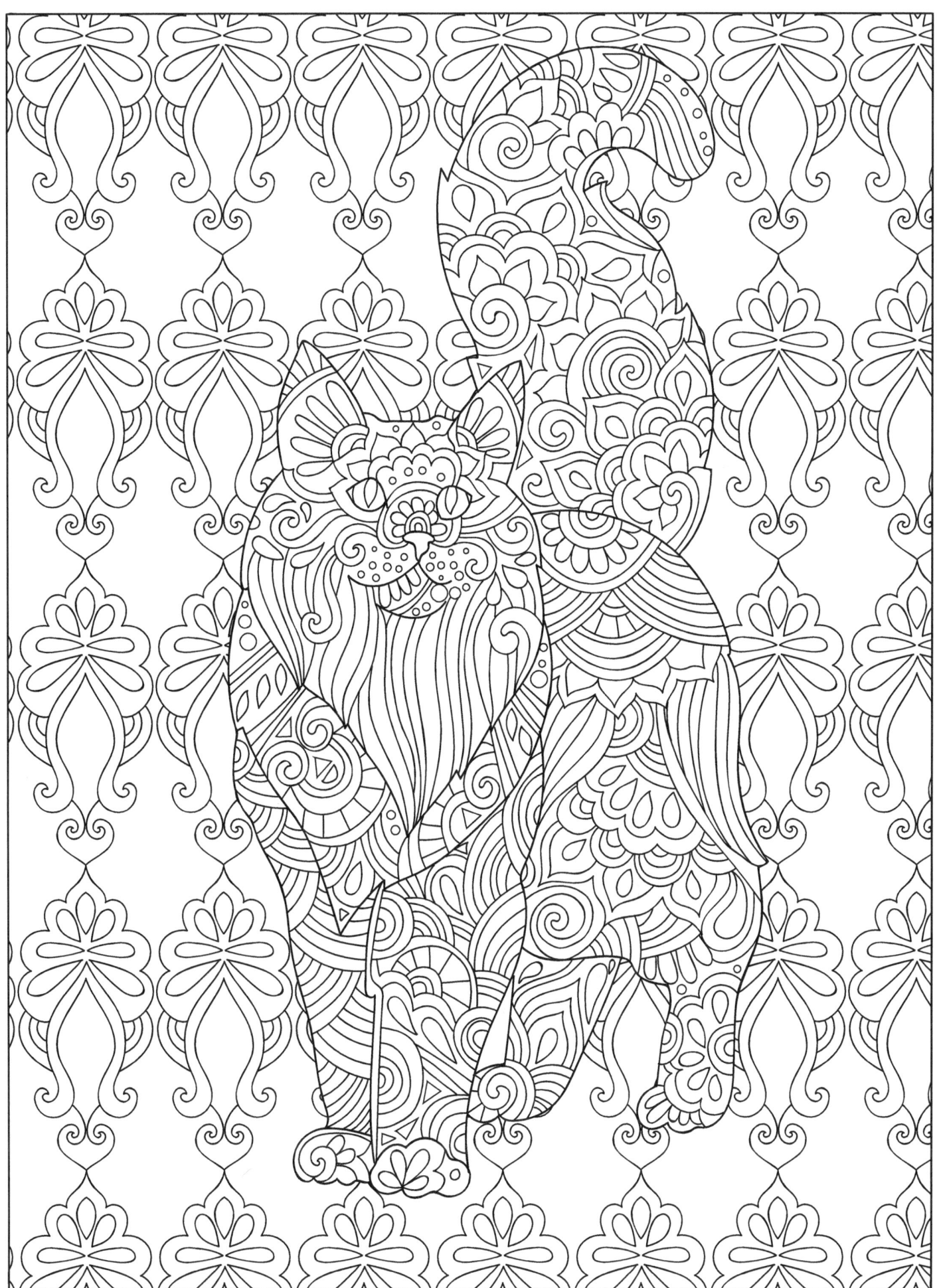

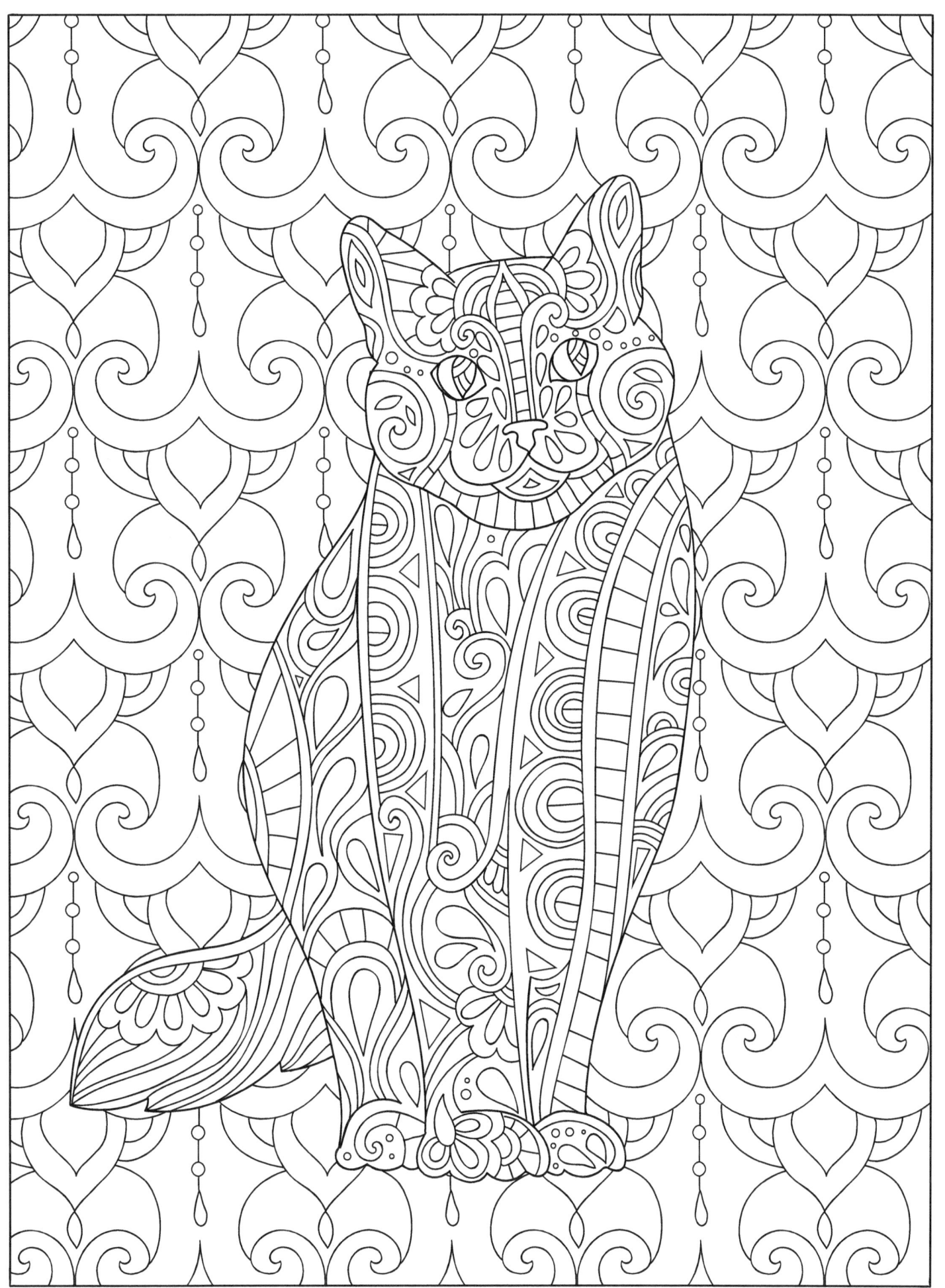

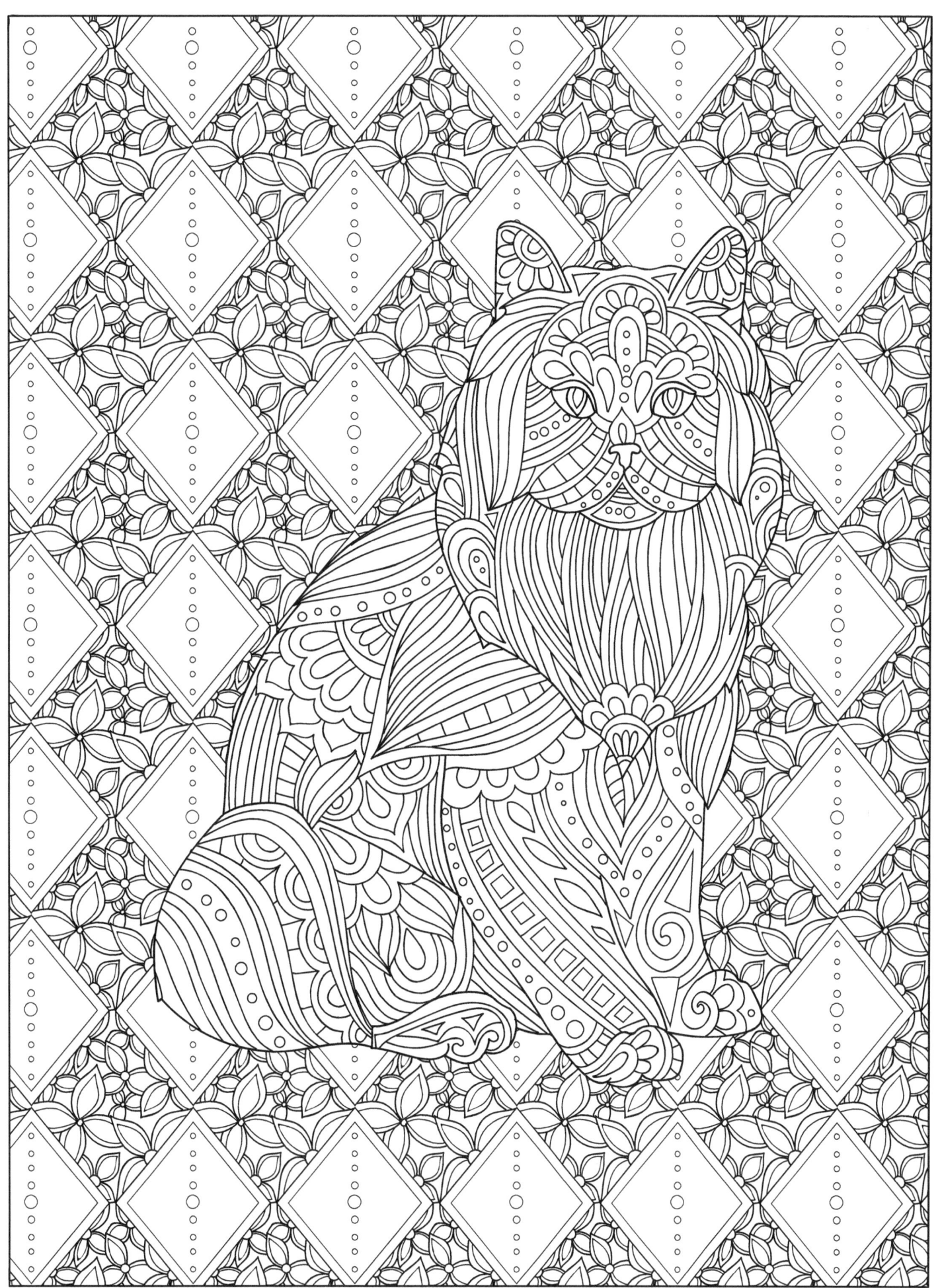

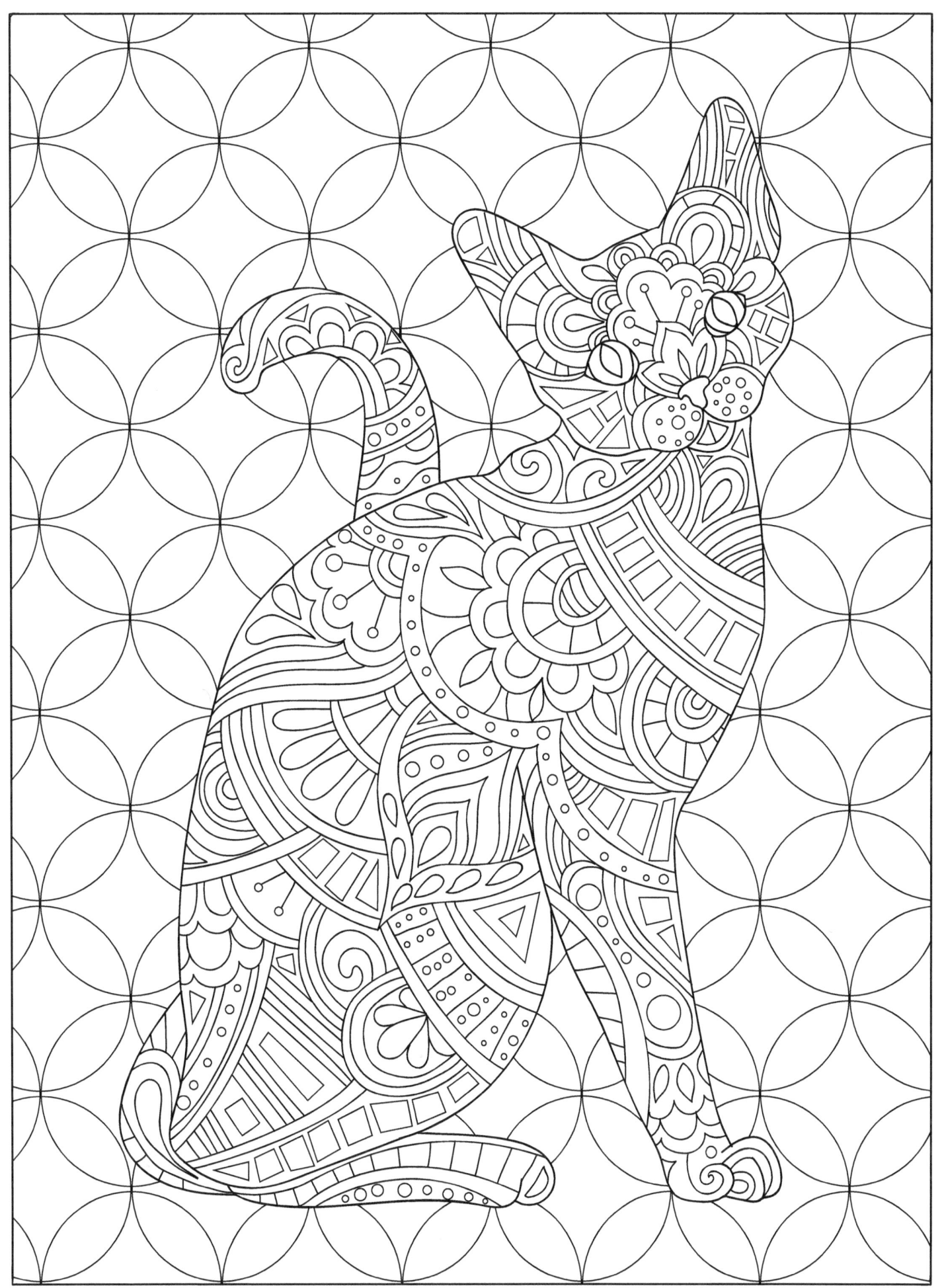

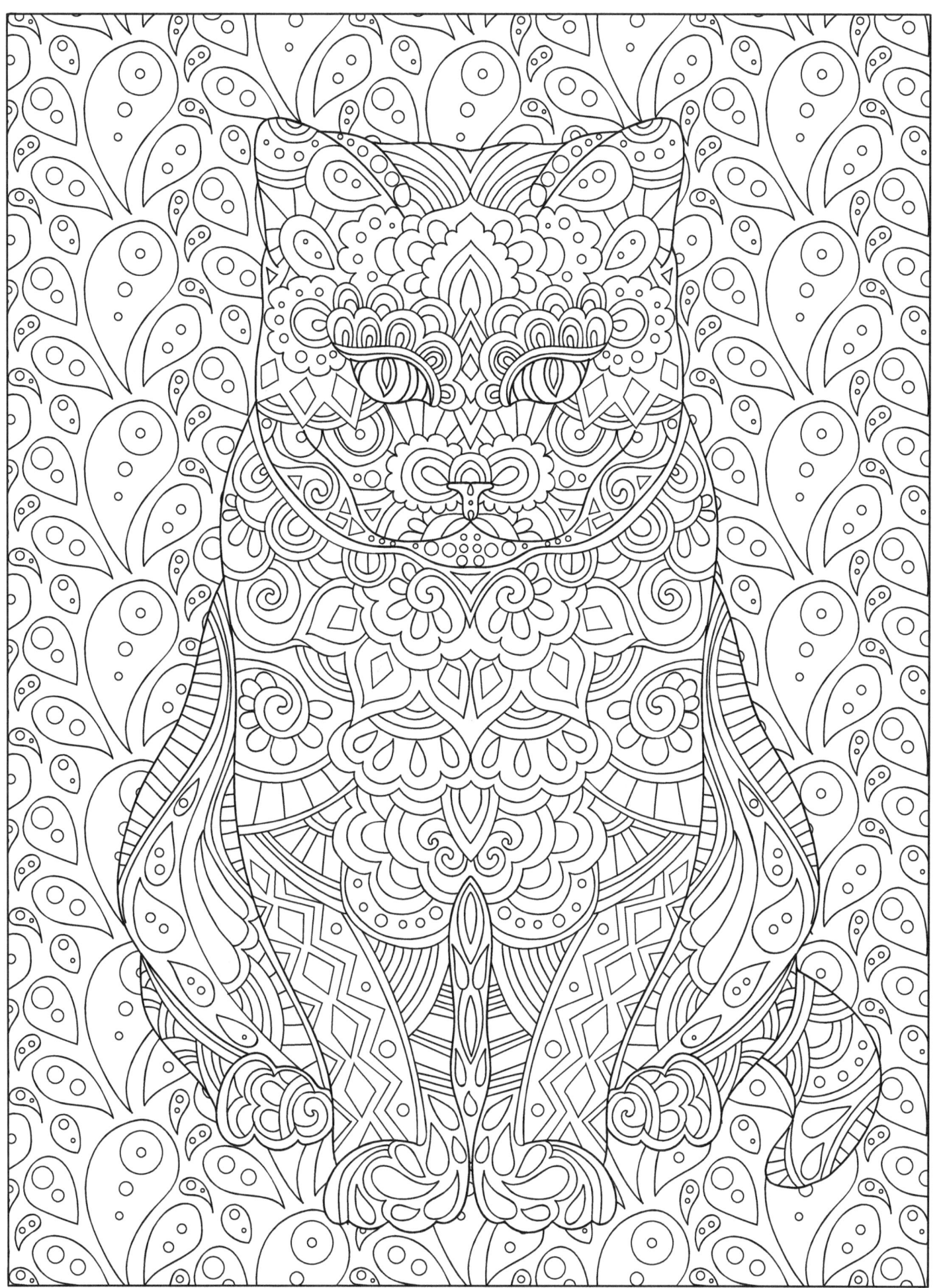

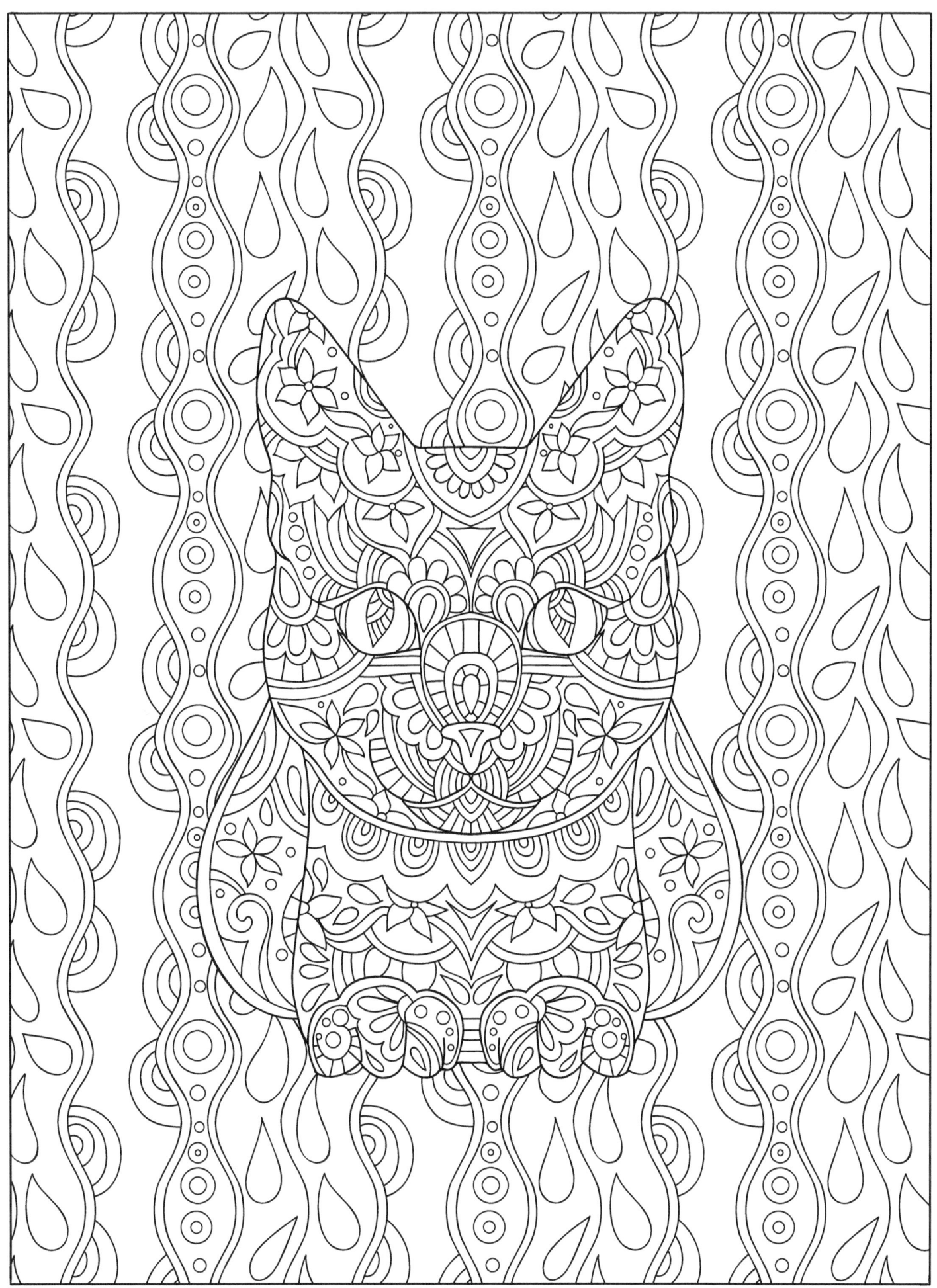

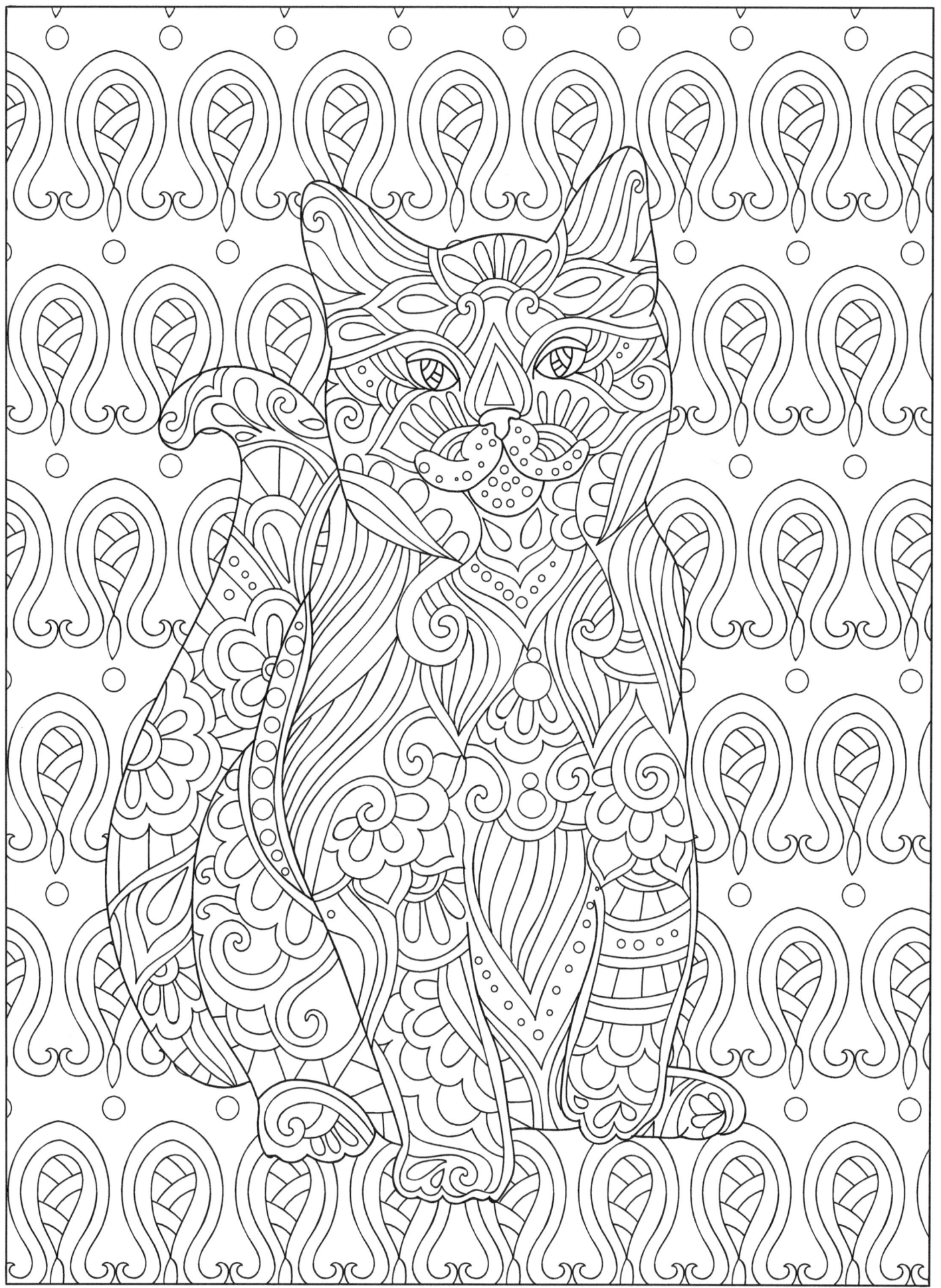

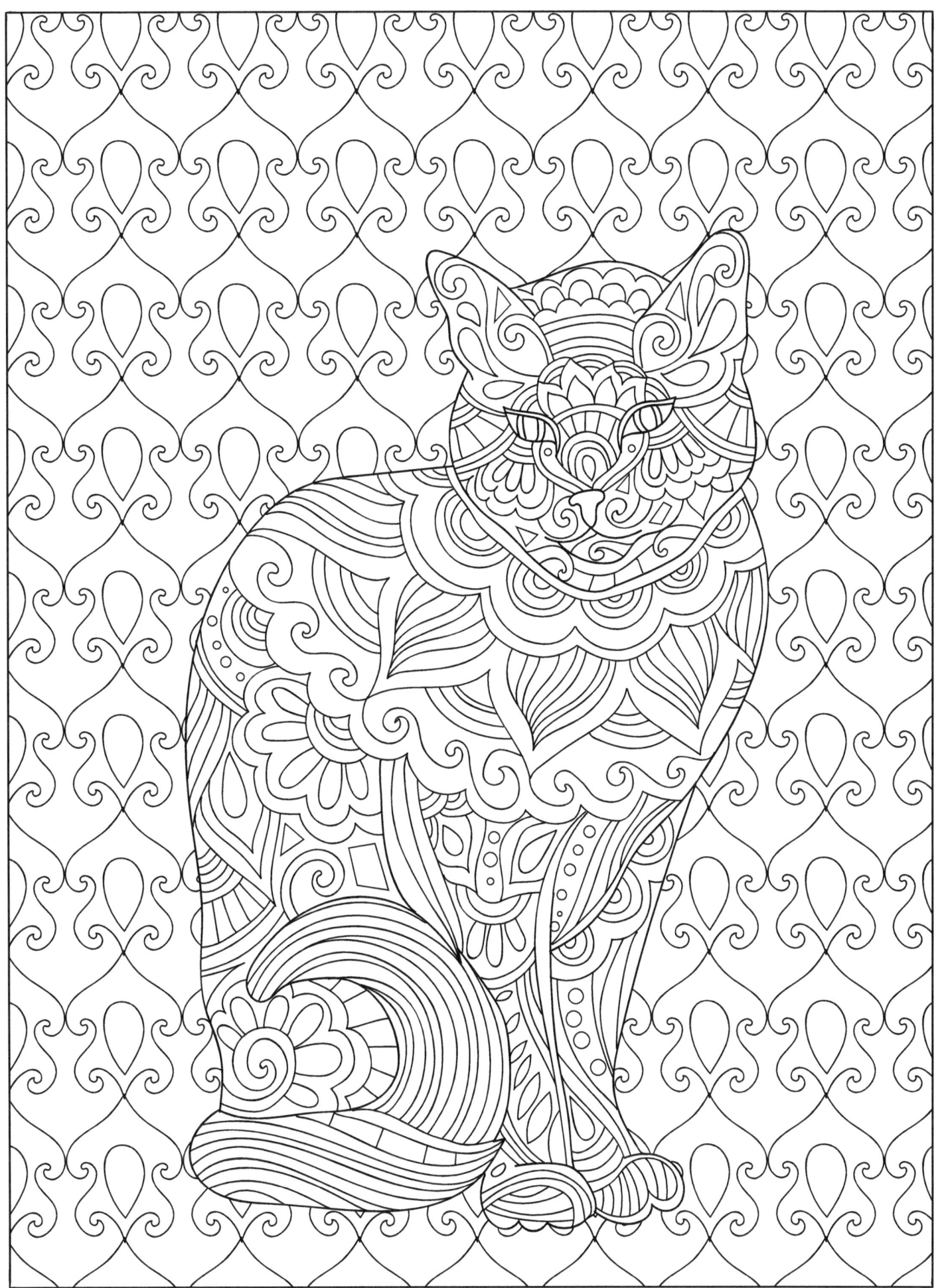

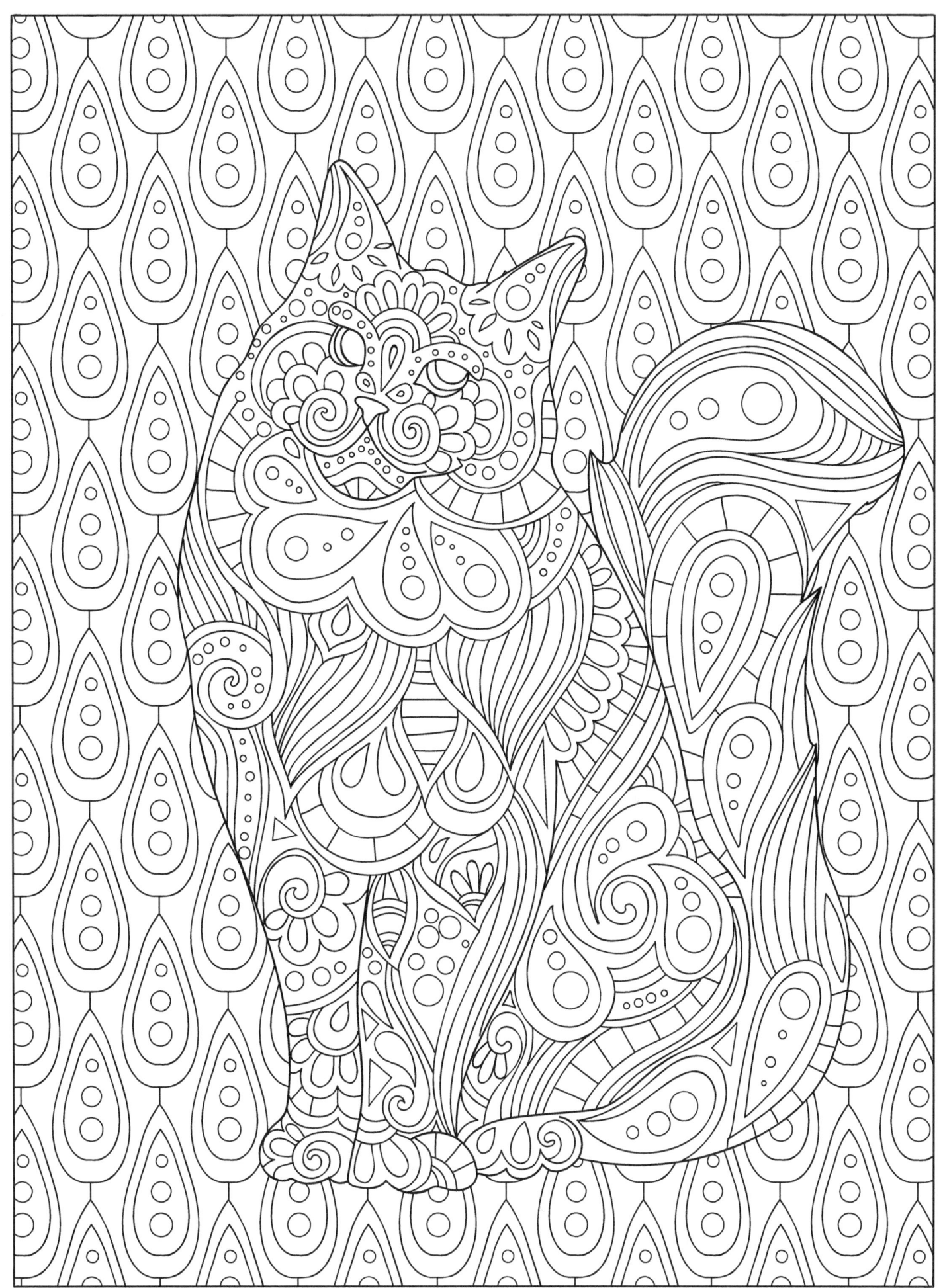

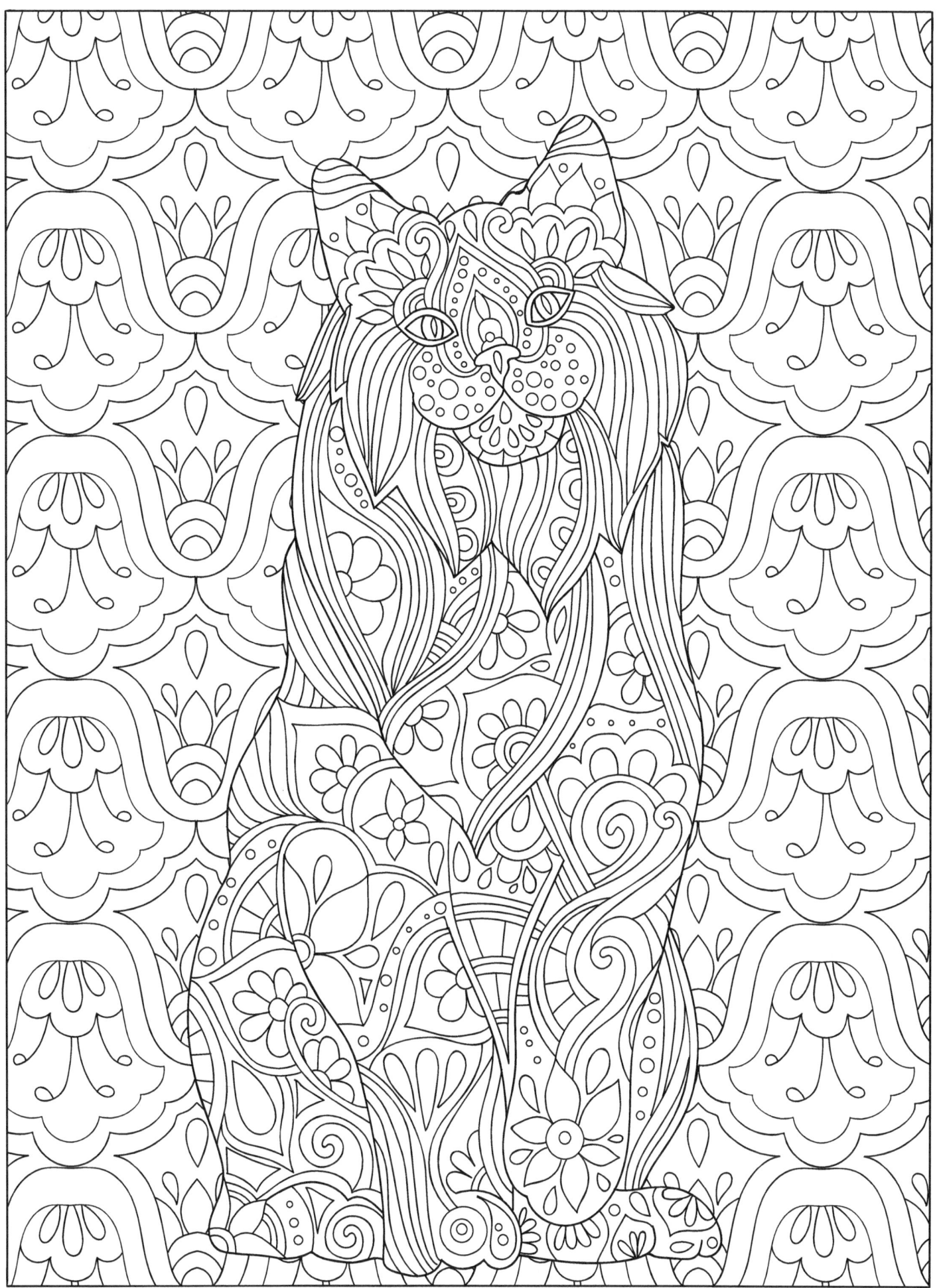

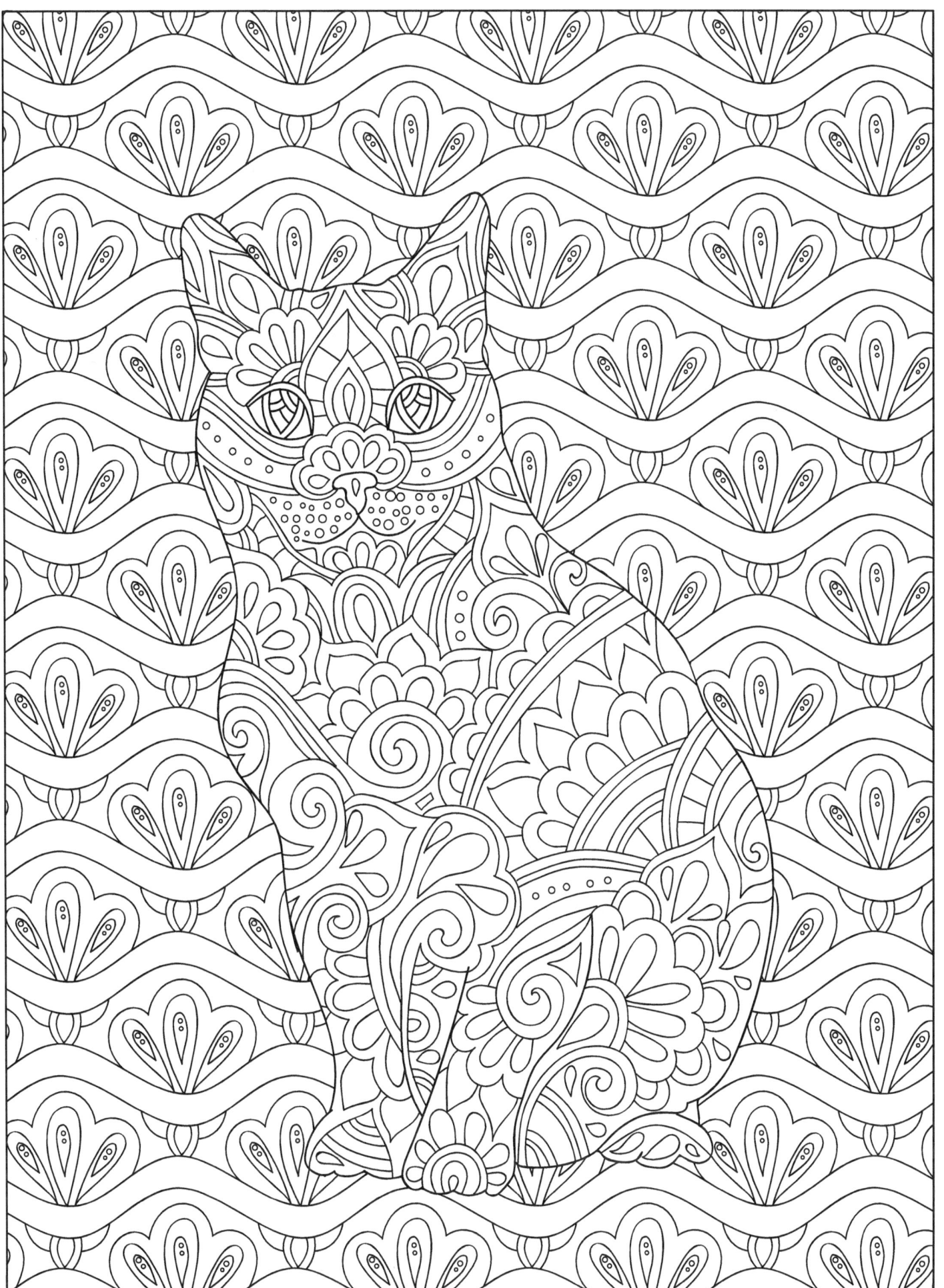

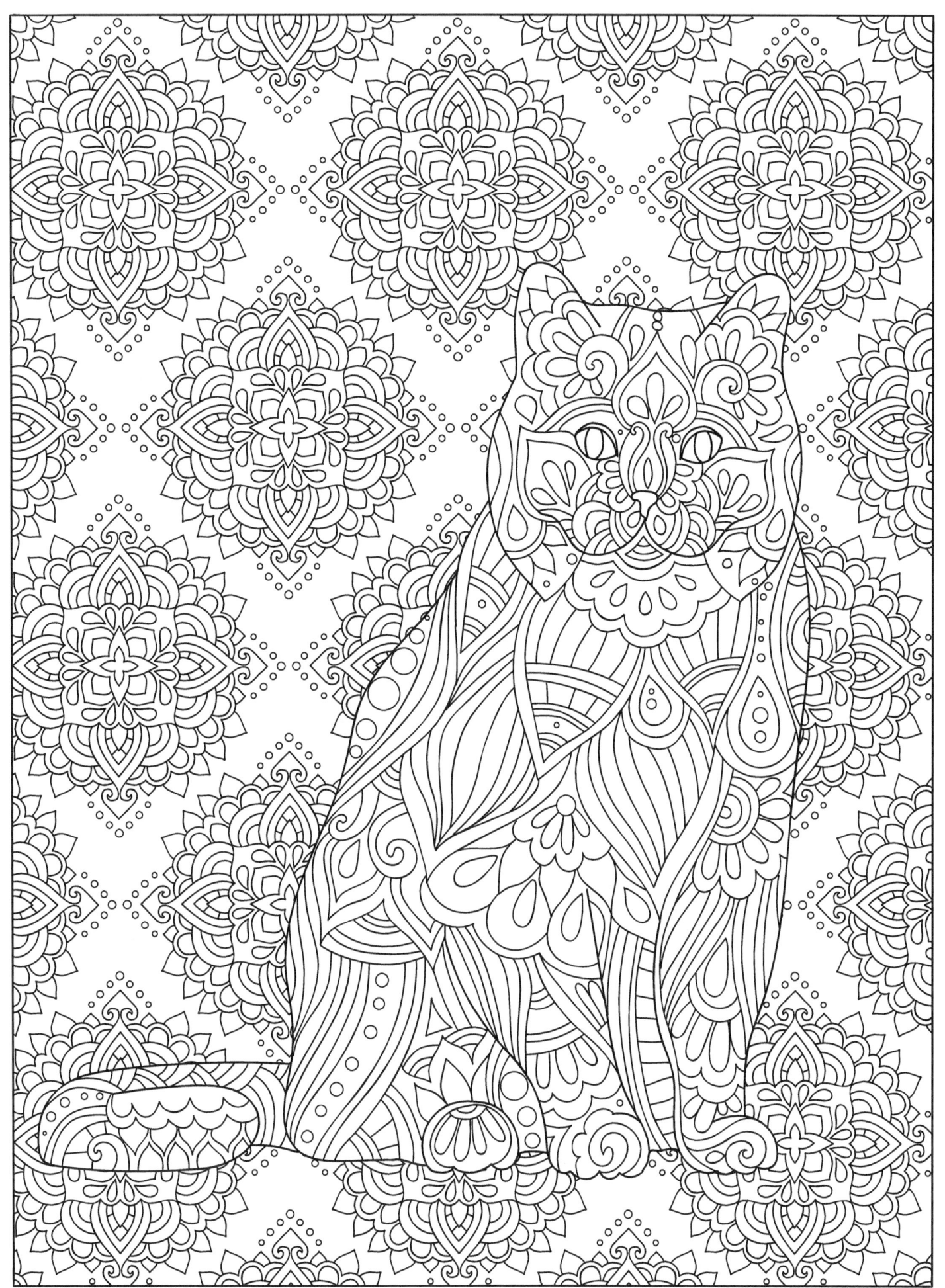

www.ingramcontent.com/pod-product-compliance
Lightning Source LLC
Chambersburg PA
CBHW062357220526
45472CB00008B/1842